Will De Grasse

Swallows on the Wing

A Medley of Prose and Verse

Will De Grasse

Swallows on the Wing
A Medley of Prose and Verse

ISBN/EAN: 9783744692052

Printed in Europe, USA, Canada, Australia, Japan

Cover: Foto ©Thomas Meinert / pixelio.de

More available books at **www.hansebooks.com**

SWALLOWS ON THE WING

O'ER

GARDEN SPRINGS OF DELIGHT;

𝔄 𝔐𝔢𝔡𝔩𝔢𝔶 𝔬𝔣 𝔓𝔯𝔬𝔰𝔢 𝔞𝔫𝔡 𝔙𝔢𝔯𝔰𝔢.

BY

WILL DE GRASSE.

" The more thy glories strike my eyes
The humbler I shall lie ;"
For it is pride that only prevents happiness ,
" Thus while I sink my joys shall rise
Immeasurably high."

NEW YORK :
PUBLISHED BY MICHAEL DOOLADY,
No. 448 Broome Street.
1866.

PREFACE.

The title of this *bouquet* of summer recreation, under the name of

"SWALLOWS ON THE WING,"

may suggest to some minds reminiscences of that charming piece of music known under the name of "When the Swallows Homeward Fly," one of Schubert's most charming songs. To others it may seem typical of the flight of those summer guests who skim o'er the watering-places of the north, and, not unlike Gideon's followers, lap the waters only to slake their thirst while in the pursuit of those transitory pleasures which a hot summer compels us all to seek. The additional term of "Garden-Springs of Delight" may hint at the cursory character of mere pleasure-seekers, who hop from spring to spring, passing over the real delights which are contained in the inner light of natural beauty, but do not stop to consider that our strength lies often in sitting still, after the old Italian proverb, *Quieta non movere.*

"The rolling stone gathers no moss," and a hop, skip, and jump, after the manner of boys playing at hop-scotch, is no less typical of the leap-frog processions of those rapid travelers who race from Land's End to the Falls of Niagara, or from Penobscot to Milwaukie, as if life and death depended on the measure of their velocity. The habit is so general that it has become contagious. It is the fashion, and that is the end of it. Nature now has no further use than to supply artificial waterfalls for those natural. Gardens are turned into illustrations for the beauties of the fall bonnets; cataracts are delicately converted into rats and mice, which lie dormant under the hair: and all nature is swallowed up in a fearful distortion of fire principles, not unlike the Duke of Bridgewater's Treatise, in which he proclaimed " that rivers were made to feed cana's." Thus it happens that swallows become gulls, beauties are turned into beaux, and all the springs of life so twisted out of shape that our carriages ought to be *dragged*, for we are all going too rapidly downhill. Finally, it comes to this, that the grave swallows us all. While time is on the wing, we are all passing through garden-springs of delight, if we did but know it. The elastic spring of " her little feet beneath her petticoat, like little mice, run in and out, as if they feared the light," and the steel spring of Brooks' handsome boots, which Adam's offspring delight to display every day on Broadway, is but an offset to show off the flaunting wings and plumage of birds-of-paradise and pheasant, which adorn the head-dresses of all the she-swallows that flit along our streets. Notwithstanding which we have to swallow them whole, and are ingulfed in such a maelstrom of delight that we men cannot possibly escape from their influence, even should we use our swallow coat-tails as rudders to weather out their storms.

God bless and preserve all the women,
But allow a few rights for their men !—Adieu !

REMINISCENCES OF STOWE.

A SKETCH OF A

SUMMER TRIP THROUGH VERMONT.

BOOK FIRST.

WHEN a man in a boat rows one way and looks another, he is not unlike certain people who go into the country on a pleasure excursion for the avowed purpose of enjoying themselves, or improving their health, during a period of one, two, or three months, according to their fancy. What a strange result often succeeds their aspirations after these various ends ! How often have the many fond imaginations of travelers or sojourners throughout the country been thrust aside, and led them to misgivings, as to whether the original design of each individual had been carried out to the full extent of their programme !   •

Mr. and Mrs. Plumpkins intended, perhaps, to save board ; for, when you move in May from the city, it is just as economical to board in the country for six months as to keep a hotel for your negro servants in the metropolis, just as the English go to Bologne for economy's sake

Jamaway and family, with three small children and one at the breast, find it best to pass away the heated term of the year, and enjoy their pastime, near the marble quarries of Vermont.

Jones and family, having sent their carriages and teams ahead with Jenkins, their coachman, may choose Saratoga as the best place to do their summerings at this present rowdy and shoddy resort of fashion and *extravagance.* What cares Publican Franks whether the *élite* longer frequent his *caravansera* or not, so long as Bill Longdraft comes to inhabit his rooms, and is willing to stable his four-in-hand in his barns, and open his six bottles of champagne a day at the table d'hôte? Such, however, is life at Saratoga now; and the place where the world, the flesh, and the devil go is the spot where our saints like best to study out the warnings of the preachers; where all are so well exhibiting the everchanging contrast between the lights and shadows of life. Whichever watering-resort is sought, by whomsoever, and among whomsoever, it matters not; the same things always happen, "that people do not do the thing they first pretended to when they left their homes for to do." All seem to be trying their utmost to make themselves as miserable as possible during the hot weather; and, instead of going up the mountains to reside there during the interval of their absence, they remain under the porches of an inn, always complaining about the heat, or frying their complexions in the sun, and getting pretty well roasted out in the air in a hot valley, quite snugly ensconced between the adjacent hills, so that they get so well baked by the time they are ready to go home that you would think

that they had been all the time basted with flour, put in
a Dutch tin roaster, and had been so well cooked that
they would keep well preserved all through the winter,
so very well had they been done brown. " Verily, this
is stepping out of the frying-pan into the fire."

For instance, we quote the present game of croquet,
so furiously engaged in by the ladies, with an occasional
beau for a partner, for the men were so scarce this summer in these regions that they could not be had for love
or money, even by advertisement, excepting a few super-
annuated old bachelors, who boasted they had passed
seventeen years successively at Sharon, Saratoga, and
White Mountains. What a wonder that the waters and
the snows from the mountains had not completely washed
them out of the way! But notwithstanding all this,
travel is a mixed matter, and all of us being but passen-
gers in this wilderness of life, like the whole fabric of
these human bodies, it has its warp and woof of contra-
diction, folly, and delight. A little health is the gain, a
little pain sometimes in the heart; the gain is flirta-
tion, poetry, song, festivity ; and heart-burn from sorry
victuals and bad cooking ; and amid all the crowds that
are hurrying back and forth through the mazy intervals
of valleys, water-courses, and waterfalls, life is not unlike
a rapid stream which is swiftly flowing and wending its
course toward the broad ocean of eternity.

Ever and anon the dream is broken by accident, and
sad catastrophes mingle among the course of our summer experience ; for example, one fair damsel has a fall
and breaks an ankle on Mount Monadnock's slippery
side, and is carried down the hilly path, straddled
a-pig-back, held up by her attendant gallants, the

only and a novel mode of constructing a stretcher for the broken limb. Another youthful girl is accidently shot by a pistol carelessly handled by her lover, at Conway, New Hampshire. Two fair beauties from Gotham are thrown out of a buggy, the harness having broken, and themselves saved from a pitch over the precipice, but are rescued from destruction by the strong arm of the gallant *Miles*, a soldier of civic fame in Brattleboro'. Not far off a sad murder is committed in a barn at Williston, by some returning stray soldiers of fortune. A barrel of gold was the prize which satan held out to tempt their avarice ; but there was retribution in the sacrifice of this victim, for covetousness had early seized the brain of this greedy woman, who had boasted that she would never be satisfied until she had got her barrel of gold ; she was killed in the same barn where the money had been hidden for years, and long before her secret had been disclosed, as it was heard by a wily listener. It was just the devil breathing the poison in the woman's ear, as in the old time of Adam.

Again we are shocked by rumors of certain moral falls, and sad catastrophes breathe through the air of far-off Gotham. The sulphurous taints of Sodom and Gomorarrah reach our ears through the channels of the daily press, while non-residents are startled by the iniquities of Jenkins and the constructive gold forgeries of poor young Ketchum. As for ourselves, our peace of mind was too valuable, and no newspaper was suffered to disturb the entire period appointed for our fixed episode for rest and repose. " No news being good news," as saith the proverb, why bother about things which do not concern you ? as for bad news, it flies quick

9

enough. But to return to the course of travel, let us go back, as one is often compelled when starting horses on the race-course.

At our departure from New York, in July, we took the Daniel Drew (not having first stopped to enquire how much she drew). We had first been interrupted by a policeman ordering our baggage-wagon off the dock (city ordinance requiring all private carts should be licensed) ; it was thought best to apologize and pocket the affront, and we promised that in future the family name should be properly and fully painted both on our cart and on our donkey. We had a very pleasant sail as far as Albany, and nothing further occurred to interrupt the journey until a baggage-man, purporting to be the regularly appointed expressman for the Drew, seized hold of our escort just as we were about landing at the steamboat wharf, and, taking the list of our several pieces of baggage, gave us his address on a card, having the number of the checks which he had placed on each of the trunks ; these we retained, and without further anxiety, having been assured by this factor that we need not be at all concerned about its delivery at the cars, we took an omnibus, and started in great haste, in order to take the train which was about to start for Saratoga from the depot near the Delavan House (for there was just five minutes time to be spared in this hurry). We had been reassured that the luggage would follow by the next train, which was to leave at 7, P. M.—it was now 5, P. M., and that we would find it all safe at Saratoga.

On our arrival at the Clarendon Hotel, kept by one of the Lelands, we secured rooms for the ladies, but

1*

after inquiring after the trunks, none were forthcoming
What a predicament for a party of ladies to be left in !
They might as well have been left without waterfalls,
crinoline, or money-bags. In traveling dress it was
very difficult to present ourselves in the society of the
parlors of the various hotels, but one could peep in at
the windows and recognize a few acquaintances, who
were busily chatting and gossiping inside, and very
much engaged in discussing the characters of the hop,
at which they were expected to enjoy themselves a
great deal, as it was to be the last ball of the season.
The pleasure of looking in through the windows, while
other people were enjoying themselves in dancing and
having a good time generally, is not unlike that which
Dickens tells of, where a boy is supposed to view an
operation through the front glass of an apothecary's
shop window while the surgeon is cutting off a man's
leg in the back room, out of sight; or like that peculiar
burst of indignation which falls from a near-sighted person, who drops his spectacles, and is stopped, stone blind,
in the middle of the crisis of a very stirring novel which
he had been engaged in reading. In short, there was
nothing in it, as Matthews observed after he had walked
up Vesuvius and looked down the crater, "There was
nothing in it after all." The fun, like the fiery lava, was
all outside, so there was nothing for the Fudge party to
do but to retire to the hotel, and go to bed that night to
dream of the lost trunks which were expected to arrive
the next day.

On the next morning search for the baggage was
resumed. No trunks were found even after having dis-
patched a telegraph and a special messenger. So, after

having attended the races, our party started by an express train named for that occasion the *race-train*. We arrived late in the afternoon back at Albany, and there found all our light baggage snugly ensconced in the freight depot in charge of the baggage-master, where it had been held for safe keeping, and for the express purpose of getting an extra quarter of a dollar for every piece of *inpedimentum* owned by each member of our party. Make a note of this, and chalk it down as " *Swindle No. 1.*" *Stick a pin here.* The next beautiful experience that occurred to the Fudges was in our dealings with the agent of that new arrangement which has been started recently, at an office near Stanwix Hall, in a rear building, which is denominated " *The Troy and Boston Railroad : the old and reliable all-rail route.*" Here you take your tickets through, and as our party were bound for Manchester, in order to visit the Equinox Mountains, we were ticketed through to that point by one Mr. Craven, agent, by name; the baggage was properly marked, and the two ladies' money-bags were checked as one piece ; this was expressly so directed by said agent, and performed under the eye of their escort and in presence of the hotel porters. This piece of caution having been secured, our party started by the city railroad cars, and, having passed over the bridge, were ferried across the Hudson to the city of Troy opposite. It were well to describe the little ferry-boat which plies between this point and Troy. Imagine a very respectable large-sized washtub to which paddles have been attached, and that an inconceivably small cabin-like shed had covered over a large tea-kettle which keeps puffing away under a high pressure of steam with the furiousness of an enraged porpoise, and that the whole machine went sputtering through the water with a velocity and a bluster quite disproportionate to the size of the machine, and you will have but a poor idea of the little sea-monster which plows through the water, near these Trojan banks, on the Hudson, and which has no *simile* to express its peculiar features, not even in those little black steam-tugs which ply on the Thames, between Westminister and Waterloo bridge, in London.

We had no sooner landed in Troy, and taken our seats in the cars on the Troy side of the river, when we discovered that one of the small bags of the party had been cut away by one of the light-fingered gentlemen who frequent the depots of every city, and like birds of prey follow after the trunks of travelers. N. B.—We are happy to say that, after several telegraphs and sundry strong epistolary notes, savoring of a smack of the legal profession, the lost small bag was duly forwarded to the owner thereof at Boston. We do, in justice to the agent's efforts, thank Mr. Craven for its expedition to our friend's address on Chestnut street.

BOOK SECOND.

MANCHESTER VILLAGE, VERMONT.

Whatever other people may say of the delightful climate of the STREET of Manchester, in Vermont, for such is the title by which non-resident and *town* folks in the vicinity designate this plot of habitation, we found it one of the hottest plains in Vermont, situated in an interval (for valleys are so entitled in this region). It is embraced within the two ranges of hills which hem it in ; the Green Mountains on the easterly side, and the Equinox Mountain on the westerly slope. Why don't people call things by their proper names? Were it not for the numerous marble quarries, yielding their product of calcareous chalk or blocks of white marble, derived from them after they have been wedged out of their strata, there is scarcely a range of elevation in the State of Vermont, excepting Mount Mansfield, near the village of Stowe, which is truly worthy of the name of "a mountain." Truth demands that they should be always called what they were first named, "The Green Hills of Vermont"—*Ver* being a contraction of *verdi*—which ancient conglomerate settled down into such a green mixture of graywacke, gneiss, granite, hornblende, and into cold marble, so shocked its barefaced neighbor, old Mountain Equinox, that nature filled its interior with a basis of slate in sheer opposition, which could not possibly be construed into anything

like green, even should any strolling artist designate it
green among his pencilings in slate-pencil. In fact,
old Equinox was so jealous of its own mountainous
characteristic that it denied having any connection
with the Green Hills, and, taking refuge among the spurs
of the Adirondack chain, positively refused to permit
any of the Vermonters to quarry out its veins, but sent
to Wales for Welshmen to substantiate its own con-
sciousness of superior rank as a respectable mountain.
Notwithstanding this little digression, which served to
while away our stay at this point, we can say that they
keep a very fair table at the hotel on the *Street*, and our
hostess, Mrs. Orvis, did everything to make our visit
agreeable to our party. The rides about the place are
quite numerous and pretty, and can all be done after
dinner ; the most charming are those which run along
in sight of, and on the borders of, Batten kill, the most
notable stream ever distinguishable among these hills,
which once had plenty of trout in its waters, but now
has been too often trolled out by the thousands of fishermen who frequent this country village. During the
summer the guests of the hotel are privileged, however, to try their skill and fish on the Orvis artificial
pond, near by, provided their product is placed in the
larder of the hotel. On the whole, this is a good place
to kill time in, and to escape from the corrupt influences
of the city ; or, as the Italians say, one's " *villiagiatura* "
might as well be passed at Manchester as elsewhere,
on the principle that ice is better kept when covered up
with a blanket than by any other means, and provided
that your inn is well kept, house room, swept nicely, and
your Boniface a good fellow ; warm-natured people

might as well be settled down near these quarry store
of white marble, and cool off under the shadow of these
hills, on the same principle that one looks on snow to
dream of Caucasus.

The ascent to Equinox Mountain was attempted by a
couple of our guests on horseback, but, as we are not
in the habit of telling more of those travelers' tales
than the truth permits, we will only say th:.t we did not
get up to the summit, but stopped short at the ruins of
an old block-house, that might as well have been called
a log-cabin, for sheltering parties, and having plucked
a fir-tree from its bed among the rocks (which still, as
planted by us, is to be seen at the house of the Rev. Dr.
W——, an old preceptor of one of our party—a memento
of our failure, but a monument for a future visit), we
left the summit behind us, thus saving us several
hundred yards of hard climbing ; and stretched before
us is that sweet perspective of distance which lends
enchantment to the view. Rapidly descending the sides
of the mountain, we arrived back at the hotel, having
gathered for our compensation the following reflections :
That we did not see the view which might have been
sighted if the hot misty sky had not prevented us ;
that all we did see was a fine view of the valleys down
below, which were sprinkled with numerous farm-
houses, presenting an appearance of landscape which
resembled mere patches of bed-quilts, such as are
worked into the varied party-colors of a country bed-
quilt or a rag carpet ; and the best part of the journey
up was repaid by those glimpses of scenery which are
seen as you ascend and look through the openings in
the forests, whence you obtain such pictures, along the

ruuning line of the hills, the aspects of the distant mountains, the rapid lifelike, rocky, rilly streams, and the far-off villages, which present to the beholder such sketches of landscape and patches of beauty, interminglings of shadows and light, cloud phantoms and sunshine, as convey to the artist those emotions that form his ideas for studies, to be finished up and furnished to the life at home in his studio. Apart from these there is naught worthy of notice except an occasional pleasant conversation with an old friend, seen in a new aspect, the forming of new acquaintances, and a few happy comparisons and criticisms with the artist alongside of you. It is not worth while saying anything of the fancy ball which we did not see, and if we had we might have been tempted to say some foolish things about the follies of the fair, and the fantasies of one graceful lady who advertised *Sterling's ambrosia* in a more extensive manner than had ever been before; but of the rest "the least said the soonest mended." There is a pretty little Episcopal church at Factory village, many very intelligent people in the place, many warm, earnest hearts beating with all those ardent feelings that dwell eternally in the human breast ; and we enjoyed our time spent there for Sabbath rest with benefit to our souls, and listening to the sound of—

Church bells, beyond the stars heard—the soul's blood —
The land of spices—something understood ;
And in prayer, the Church's banquet—angel's age ;
The soul in paraphrase ; the heart in pilgrimage.
The Christian's plummet, sounding heaven and earth,
God's breath in man returning to his birth.

—GEORGE HERBERT.

While there one of our party left for an excursion to Lake Memphramagog. It was a hurried journey, occupying three or four days, one of which was spent on our return at Bellows Falls, of which place more will be said anon. It will be observed in travel that "they who know least about a place are the first to deter you from going to see it," and that there are a hundred different opinions about every point which is to be visited, and every place to stop at on your road. One says, "Don't go to Stowe, it's so *stupid;*" others say, "Don't go to Bellows Falls, they'll run you down on the Falls;" another says, "Don't go to Brattleboro', there is no water-cure there now," and so on *ad infinitum.* Our best advice is to go in spite of all that other people say. There are always some kind people who are ready to say, as they did to *Eothen,* "Don't go to Cairo, there were two men of the same name as yourself who died there of the plague." "Don't go to Spain," was said to another party, "the banditti will murder you." In spite of which we did go, and had a very pleasant time in both places. The chances in travel are those of the sailor with the cannon ball. Two balls don't often go through the same hole, and the old fable sums up the whole matter in a nutshell : " If you want to dance, you must pay the fiddler ; " and again, " It is not proper in any case for an old man to carry the donkey on his shoulders when he has sons who have broad backs."

Now that the railroad is finished up to the shore, it was found best to go to Lake Memphramagog this summer, leaving Bellows Falls for another time. Mr. S——, of Baltimore, joined me in this excursion, and in spite of all that was told us about the horrid hotel at White

River Junction, we pushed on northward by way of the Patumpsic and Connecticut Railroad.*

You pass several places of interest on the way to the lake. At Wells river you may take the railroad as far as Littleton, in the direction of the White Mountains, and further on, getting out, you may stage it from Bruce's Station, where one will find it will repay a digression by a trip to Lake Willoughby, which is so wild and dark. Most picturesque and gloomy are the high walls which hem in the contour of this sheet of water; a scene for a romance might be well founded from a spot which presents so bold and fearful an aspect to the vision of an imaginative traveler. And further on as you proceed, there is a little lake at about seven miles from the greater Magog, where the walls of a bold limestone formation frown over the scene, and the lofty parapets of stone present a fine aspect to the beholder as he is riding by. While approaching the end of our trip we were again warned by some fellow-traveller not to take the little boat which plies from the lake shore to Owl's Head. "It was an old canal-boat placed on wheels," said a returning volunteer, whose evidence proved of very little value on examination, for he had not been near the spot for a number of years; "and doubtless," replied the elder of our party, "all the people who have been steaming on this boat since the first of July were drowned, without benefit of clergy." It was the old

---

* This hotel during the war had been the resort of all the bounty-jumpers, and of course they left a very bad reputation behind them. But we were batchelors; we could stand it for one night. We would not advise parties with ladies to stop over here. We found the beds were clean, and the bedrooms well furnished.

story of the old man, his sons, and donkey. Don't carry it. We were bound to go. "Let us be drowned together," replied my friend ; and we did start by this steam-tug, shortly after dining at the hotel, which is capitally kept, not inferior to any other at which we had stopped during the summer. To Owl's Head we went, in spite of all ominous predictions to the contrary and found the smallest conceivable sized boat in the world was to carry about thirty people as far as this little mountain, which seemed from the wharf about seven miles distant. While you are on the way you cross the domains of her British Majesty the Queen, and while the captain was obliged to hand the ship's manifest to one of her officers, we surveyed the proportions of the custom-house, which was constructed of pine boards. Surely the Queen is not very handsomely represented by the buildings, which here stand for the dignity and powers of the kingdom of England, for the receipt of her revenue at this point. While those on the boat were whiling away an hour at the base of Owl's Head, we had an opportunity of rowing a farmer across the lake, and thereby had a fine view of the Smugglers' Cave, and were favored with a grand panoramic view of the whole lake. Memphramogog is one of the finest sheets of water in America, and when Canada is annexed to the United States it will be more beautiful still. But at present still waters run deep, and we must abide our time.

BOOK THIRD.

The passage back from the foot of *Owl's Head* Mountain was attended with no other incident than that of stopping a few minutes in order to procure some of the famous muscalongue trout which are caught on the lake. They are peculiar to these waters, but are rarely taken except by the most expert fishermen. We returned, by the Patumpsic and Connecticut Railroad *via* St. Johnsbury and Windsor, to Bellows Falls, to spend Sunday at the latter place, where I met one of my acquaintances of the New York bar, who was on his way to the lake; and on the Sabbath evening, after tea, we agreed to climb up the hills in front of the Island House, where we viewed together the sun as it descended behind the horizon. The lansdcape here exhibited is not to be surpassed by any other point on the Connecticut river, and not less appreciable from the summits of admiration in which it was regarded by my companion, who was here enjoying his vacation. With what pleasure we observed together, the glories of the scene before us, resting awhile at various stages in the ascent ; in fact, lying down on the grass at intervals, and at one spot admired one of the most beautiful sugar-maple trees that ever spread its arms to ornament the face of nature. Many glimpses of beauty appeared through several openings in the distance, and at every stand-point a new aspect of the rich landscape spread before us. How majestically the Connecticut wound its ribboned veins through the rich lawns of green valleys that husbanded the richly cultivated plains, and how sweetly and luxuriously swelled the rounded forms of the rolling mounds of furrowed land, more lovely than even the blushes of the declining sunset gilding the mountains, but not to be compared to the full, heaving, throbbing swells of the bosom of a beautiful woman. The whole scene recalled those sweet lines of Dr. Watts :

> " How fine has the day been, how bright was the sun,
> How lovely and joyful the course that he run ;
> But now the fair traveler comes to the west,
> His rays are all gold, and his beauties are best ;
> He paints the sky gay as he sinks to his rest,
> And foretells a bright rising again ;
> And gives a sure hope, at the end of his days,
> Of rising in brighter array.'*

Let us back out of such sentimentalism, and change from mountain to the sea. It is a long day's ride by railroad from Manchester, Vermont, over the mountains, by the way of Keene and Boston, to Rye Beach, in New Hampshire.

The new hotel at Rye Beach is nicely kept and well appointed. Fashion has claimed its halls, and the usual summer delights are to be enjoyed there, not, perhaps, always in the sea, nor in the hotel, save in the society of pleasant people ; for, after all, this sought pleasure is purchased through a thousand perturbations of heart, and amid all the throbs of active human life--the most miserable of all beings is the mere woman of the world. We enjoyed one thing only in and about this place called Rye, and that was a sail in Philbrick's yacht, from the harbor, near the Atlantic House, to the old *Boar's Head*, where in my boyhood I had fished for bright cod and dark tautog, and shot plovers in the neighboring marshes. There is pleasure on the boundless sea, and its throbbing waters filled me with glorious emotions. The heart leaps in response to the music of its summer waves ; all is sublime in the upheavings of the boundless ocean.

Return now, and *chassez* across to the regions of Waterbury, and back to Stowe, through Concord, in New Hampshire. Passing by Epping, we were detained by the crowd hurrying away from the Methodist campmeeting. The cars were full of singing men. and women, and all was cheerful as the marriage-bell until we landed at Concord. Next morning, by way of White River Junction and the Vermont Central, we reached Waterbury, about 4, P. M. ; there taking the oldfashioned coach, with *six-in-hand*, we started off for Stowe. After the first four miles, the swelling lines of hills show the approach of the more remote and loftier mountains. All the way along the line of the railroad small hillocks appear, like young children, denoting a promise of a larger growth in youth and manhood. This is continuously true until you reach Mount Mansfield, the highest point in Vermont.

We landed at the Mount Mansfield Hotel at 7 o'clock, P. M., which is kept by a Company, the presiding genius of which is a counselor-at-law, one Bingham, and Bowman, his attorney, in fact. All professions, therefore, may find themselves at home here, where one is well kept, and boarded very cheap ; for people have a conscience in the town of Stowe, as we found by our own experience—*experientia docet*, such is the wisdom of the sage Solomon, often learned by hard knocks and rough railroad travel. Now we are in it for a fortnight, let us settle down into a systematic review of the pleasures and pastimes, recreations and delights, to be enjoyed at Stowe. Many years ago one Huntington and a party of artists were strolling among the mountains of Vermont in search of the picturesque, and equally as ready to draw a sketch as to take a fish out of the many trout streams which abound in the vicinity of Stowe. (Trout are very scarce there now, and can only be caught with the lure of a silver hook.) But amid the wilds and unopened paths of these mountains, some-how or other, these wanderers had lost their way, and when by chance they afterward discovered it, it was but to bivouac in the nearest farm-house, where they *stowed* their luggage, and thence yclept this name of *Stowe.*

In order to give a good idea of the many ways in which to beguile your time at this place, begin with the rides, which are the Notch ; up Mount Mansfield to Morristown Falls, and its rapids, resembling somewhat Trenton (embracing, that is, Hyde Park) ; Glen Falls view ; the lake on Elmore Mountain ; the drive to Nebraska, over the Notch, and back ; the excursion round Mansfield, and back by way of Cambridge, home ; the Bingham waterfall, recently opened, and several delightful points to be visited, even if one varies the excursion by a trip over "Hogback" to Watertown, and thence to Montpelier. Air, open-air exercise, *out* in the sunshine, or, even on the hottest day, riding on horse-back, walks afoot, walkings in company, moonlight

excursions, and its romantic attendants, poetry and
song, constitute the means of recreation, and are the
proper ways by which to establish your health. Don't
be afraid of the sun ; light, air, and freedom in the use of
your arms and legs, unrestricted by tight clothing, are as
essential to mankind or women as they are to the birds,
animals, and flowers. Healthy people go here to enjoy
the real blessings of health ; sickly people can be
nursed better at home, they are not improved by rough-
ing it and dissipation, be the spot Stowe, Saratoga, or
any one of the summer watering-resorts. Do not stick
in the hotel, in the hot atmosphere of gossip, scandal,
and peevish complaint ; the worst of victuals are good
enough for splenetic temperaments, and there are hos-
pitals for diseased minds and disordered bodies. But
go out, enjoy everything with a freshness of apprecia-
tion, and play at croquet, even with the hot sun blazing
over your head, and never mind people who are
always grumbling about the hot weather, which, if not
firmly resisted, will entirely prevent you from ever getting out of the hotel, and deprive you of very many
pleasant excursions.

On the whole, many are the delights of Stowe. All
the praises that we have heard in its favor prior to our
visit fell short of the reality of our enjoyment of the
treasures of beauty. What can exceed the grandeur of
the Notch ? the Smuggler's Notch as it is called ; the
light ascension on Barton's Rock, which crowns the end
of this valley of green, where the ribbed rocks are gar-
landed with rich verdure up to the summit of their ele-
vated bulwarks, and where, at every point of your
enraptured vision, are spread bouquets of moss-covered

boulders, which are scattered at intervals as you approach toward the fountain of the cool spring of icewater that issues out of its hidden chamber in the rocks. What more sublime than the heights of Old Mansfield's Nose, where the winds blow with the force of a hurricane, and the wild fir-trees bend their forms in homage to its majesty? The valleys lay open their beauties and fill us with admiration and delight. "We praise Thee, O God ; we acknowledge Thee to be the Lord," was the burst of our enthusiasm as we looked down on the plains below, where the vales, of gardens and fields, were fertilized by the channels of the running streams, and, standing thick with corn, make the hills rejoice on every side. Nothing can be more pleasing or invigorating than such prospects to those who relish the simple beauties of nature. We could speak of the pleasant domestic society of this admirable resort ; of the many pleasant people who really do enjoy their visit to this spot, and find that it has been good for them to have been there. The society of the parlors was more like that of the home circle, and they met together here as friends, to have a good time together. Many of the guests had been there since June ; some from Boston spend the whole summer, and gather around themselves all their relatives, who are drawn hither by the amenities of this newly discovered Utopia. We could speak of the very pleasant walks we had together ; of the Sabbath evening spent on Sunset Hill, just back of the hotel ; of the sweet music which poured from the throats of that happy band of sweet singers who sat on the rock, as the last rays of the sun, lingering still as if reluctant to depart, and of the reminiscence of the Saviour, whose love to

2

Mary and Martha led *Him* to call us all His friends, and who delighted to seek the mountain-top for prayer and meditation ; and, repeatedly, emotions of the highest gratitude arose in the midst of this group of innocent girls, as we viewed the glories of departing day.

Again, we find pleasure in the recital of the gold-hunting party, who were so cleverly grouped in the gay scenes of the *gold-washers*, by the photographer of Stowe, than whom few are more successful even in Gotham. There were also at the hotels several very good, and some distinguished, artists, among whom was the excellent President of our own Academy of Design. We will say nothing of one true lover of his art, so quiet in the study of all the natural beauties about the town and vicinity of Stowe, a proper " *Russ in urbe*," doubtless well considered and truly appreciated alongside of his companion of the easel, one Hogsdon, whose " wine needs no bush" to herald his fame. But of the singing women and graceful beauties of the parlor it becomes us not to over-praise them. Their charms are better sounded by the poets, and we leave our theme to the muse who wrote those beautiful verses which were sung by a quartette of sweet voices under the windows of the hotel at midnight, after the return of the party of excursionists who had left that morning at half-past four for St. Albans. We all appreciated the sound of music at night, and one may best understand how well we were entertained by the gushing utterance of this band of nightingales, when you are reminded by those trilling notes of a bugle on the lake, when the moonlight is shining at the zenith of ts splendor, and the solemn quiet and calm of nature s summed up in " an audible silence."

SUMMER DAYS AT STOWE.

I.

Come, comrades, join your voices
　In song before we go ;
The forest aisles will echoes ring,
　And bear the strains below.
As over us the moments pass,
　The moments lightly flow,
We'll sing, with praise of summer days,
　Of summer days in Stowe.

II.

'Neath the shadows of the mountains,
　Where the red man drew his bow,
We'll gather round the social board,
　And naught but pleasure know.
And when with reminiscences
　Our hearts are all aglow,
We'll sing, with praise of summer days,
　Of summer days in Stowe.

III.

Had this been Adam's Paradise
　Six thousand years ago,
No tempter e'er had entered in
　To fill the world with woe.
Eve would have sung her vesper hymn
　In cadence sweet and low,
As we sing now of summer days,
　Of summer days in Stowe.

IV.

Now, on the threshold of the night,
　Sol, lingering, bids us go,
And leave the homes of fairies bright
　Unvexed by foot of foe.
But let no chilling touch of time,
　While wandering to and fro,
Banish the thought of summer days,
　Of summer days in Stowe.

BOOK FOURTH.

CONTINUATION OF STOWE.

On the last evening we spent at Stowe, it was late Saturday afternoon ; we had one of the finest showers of the season; people had been praying for rain several Sundays back, and the crops were suffering for lack of moisture ; the blessing came at last, and thanksgiving, of course, followed from all the thirsty farmers. We notice this shower particularly for the reason that a large number of the guests had been caught out in the storm, some on horseback, some in buggies, others on buck-boards—a new way of riding on a spring cart, whereby a plank constitutes the seat, and a buffalo robe the saddle—others in carriages, and not a few on foot. They most all had a good ducking and came home dripping wet, more like drowned rats than the elegantly dressed ladies and gentlemen who had started out to ride. We were fortunate in having escaped this deluge, having been warned not to attempt any outside exercise, first by the appearance of the sky, and secondly by a good-natured hostler, who would not let us depart from the hotel, although we had engaged a team. But we had our compensation in going up on top of the hotel, and there remaining half an hour under the shelter of the belvedere, in the company of several ladies ; we enjoyed the glorious prospects which were there presented by various changes in the sky during the progress of the shower, and observed the numerous storm clouds in the lights and shades, which were shifting continually around the horizon; and vivid flashes as of lightning displayed the rich green belts of the bending willows waving over both banks of the Onion river, which, like a girdle of evergreen bushes, could be discovered at this point of view, as it wended its serpent-like folds throughout its whole superficial range in the perspective of the valley before your vision ; added to this was a border of the numerous mountains which fringe. the plains of Stowe, where, at one point of sight, were to be seen Mount Mansfield, Sterling Mountain, and the old bald face, Elmore Mount, the Saddle Back, Hog-back Hills, and other lofty elevations, forming a delightful picture, and perfecting one of the most gorgeous panoramas to be found in the whole extent of the Green Mountains.

On Tuesday morning we took our leave of Stowe, and stopping at Montpelier, which is one of the most interesting places in Vermont visited by us. The State house is not excelled in the elegance of its structure by any other building erected for government purposes in the United States, and only surpassed in beauty by the massive proportions of the capitol at Washington. The same architect designed both edifices. The former has been planted firmly on a rock, for its foundation was hewn out of the stony hill in its rear, upon which permanent location may it stand as long as the duration of our own noble Constitution—*Esto Perpetuo!*

Into the interior I was conducted by the amiable and Honorable Judge Noyes, who told us that he had once been a member of the Senate and of the Assembly in this State, and very courteously pointed out to us the

seat which he once occupied as a representative of his
constituents in Vermont. While in another portion of
the upper hall, he showed us a beautifully painted por-
trait of the Honorable Judge Williams, who had once
been the Chief-Justice of the State, and that this depiction of their ablest lawyer had been presented by the
members of the Vermont bar. In every portion of the
country we found it very pleasant to find this honorable
profession very ably represented ; and in spite of the
contumely with which many of us are treated, we believe
it still worthy of the respect of all fair-minded citizens.

The character of the solidarity of the Green-mountain
State is well sustained by the many specimens of
marble which are kept in the cabinet of mineralogy,
which is to be seen in the last chamber in the north
side of the lower hall. No less than one hundred and
fifty varieties of the various quarries are there collected,
and some of the samples are as beautiful and firm as
any that have been imported to this country from Italy.
They have also placed under one of the cases a very
perfect specimen of the skeleton of an antediluvian
whale, which was dug out of the marl formation
in one of the neighboring counties. In the afternoon
we took a long drive down the side of the Onion river,
and returning, after having visited the cemetery, took
a northerly direction, and followed the river road up as
far as the village of Little Barry, where, in a fine building, a very fair boarding-school for young ladies is
kept. Thence passing over the hill road, we turned
back in the direction of home, and leaving West Montpelier village, a short distance in view from our right,
we were driven through a very romantic and pictur

esque road, lately engineered alongside of the banks
of the largest branch of the Onion, where the pathway
at times seemed very hazardous, passing as it did so
closely along the bank of the stream. At these points
it seemed very wild and rapid, and flowing swiftly
rushed over the rocks in the way, and breaking at inter
vals, dashed into several very pretty cascades and
waterfalls.

It is out of the waters of this branch of the river, in the
shoals, when the water is low, that the celebrated Montpelier pearls are taken, and which can be had there at
the New York market value, and not a fraction lower.
Mr. Mead, the jeweler, to the contrary, and his Yankee
notions notwithstanding.

Why repeat any further the course of our travel afterward, when we had left Montpelier and were on our way
home by way of White River Junction and the Vermont
Central and Connecticut River Railroad, and so on, by
way of Bellows Falls to Brattleboro', where we stopped
for a fortnight's rest at this beautiful and romantically
situated town ?

Stowe has its beauties, Manchester its ; the green
pasture lands of Greenfield no less claim attention
from the artist and the poet ; but of all the places
for a poor mortal's sojourn for the summer (now that
its water-cure establishments have ceased, "let *ducks*
take to water, for 'tis their nature to") *Brattleboro'* is
our delight ; that's the spot for us, and *Apfelbaum*, our
hotel keeper, named *Appletree* in English, that social
German, is the host for us, whose house, called the
"Lawrence House," keeps itself on the German plan,
and has a sort of *laissez-aller* in its own—where everybody

does as he pleases, and of course is pleased with himself
and with everybody else, for vanity is defined by the
poet as "the sweet reflection of one's own sweet self
into the self-same image of another's mind." This Emil
Apfelbaum kept a very sloppy house. When the rattling
stage-coach landed us at the front door, we were ushered
in with our trunks, that is to say, we carried our own
trunks on our proper persons, but how the trunks ever
got off the stage and were landed in our rooms is still
a mystery to ourselves. Shortly after, we sought to find
a book wherein to register our names ; presently a tall
slim man, slipshod, and in rather shabby deshabille
walked through the entry, and saluted us, or rather we
hailed him, saying, "Do you keep this hotel ?" to which
he answered, "Ya !" We replied : "You'll find us the
very best friends in the world, and we'll be treated as if
you had known us all your life." On going up stairs
the uncarpeted floor, wearing the last stages of con-
sumption, struck our attention; passing along the entry,
an apparition floated beyond the gallery by the stairs ;
this turned out to be the amiable Irish housekeeper of
the establishment, a dumpy, rosy-faced, and fair, fat,
and forty young woman, who attended to things generally. We were led into certain small and narrow little
alcoves, misnamed bedrooms. We looked out of the windows of the gallery into the court-yard beneath; a shabby
basin for a fountain, with no water in it, stood in the middle of the court-yard ; beyond was a veranda overlooking
a stone wall, pitched two hundred feet above the river,
that river was nowhere in sight, and the whole prospect
was gloomy, and foreboded nothing of good omen.
Chambermaids were rushing around ; no water was to be

had for washing ; towels were very scarce, and very poor at that. We remained in these wretched cabins numbered, respectively, Nos. 61 and 63, and rested that night to dream only about our boots standing before the church door, and of a Dutch angel playing an impossible tune on the organ near the south transept. We couldn't stand such another night's roosting on the upper branches of this man's appletrees, and on the morrow moved down stairs, where we remained, and beating up recruits at the breakfast table, got hold of the waiter-girls and partook of a scanty meal, after which we looked around at our position, and commenced forming a circle of acquaintances to bolster up our misfortunes.

Not many days elapsed before we were feeling more at home, and in the society of several friends, some of whom we had met at Stowe, we managed to spend a very delightful time at this notable village, the last and best, as far as the enjoyment was concerned, and the *ultima thule* of our summer trip. How can we describe the beauties of the vicinity of Brattleboro? how well portray the rich verdure of its scenery ? What a sweet prospect yields to your admiration of that beautiful bend in the valley of the Connecticut, which is presented to your vision as you look out from the graveyard, or *the cemetery*, which affords such pleasant walks on a Sunday evening ! And then the rides about the town. That to West Brattleboro', where the girls exhibited their bloomer costumes in their exercises on Friday afternoon ; and of course the young gentlemen go there to admire their calisthenic drill in short bloomers. What beauties line the shores as you drive

2*

down to Hinsdale ; how glorious the drive which leads
you over Chesterfield Mountains and back, when you
view the grand panorama of the distant hills as the
sunset gilds the mountain-tops, and thence descending by the gorge and ravines which cross your
path by the side of the gulf road ; and what delights
are spread at your vision of the Bliss farm, or at the
new turn from that, over the hills, and back to town as
you wade across the West river ! No less than forty
different rides and drives over this charming country
are among its varied attractions. What can we say of
the pleasant little village church, the beautiful little
lady's church. Episcopal, so snugly located near the
banks of the river, where by soft moonlight you may
seat yourself and dream of Paradise, and of the prospects waiting for us on the golden shores of heaven :

"Old friends, old scenes, familiar grow
As more of heaven in each wo see :
Some softening gleams of love and prayer,
Shall dawn on every cross and care.
" Goerge Herbert."

Since such charming pleasure cannot be too often
repeated, as " a thing of beauty is a joy forever," we
recur to that charming drive wherein the reins were
held by the charming Laura—not Petrarch's. There
were three couples that had started together on the
bright afternoon of the last of September. Hinsdale
was again visited, but under different circumstances of
light and shade, and the charms of sweet communion
with a lovely belle of the Quaker city led us to dream of
fairy land as wo passed over hill and dale, and lingering

until twilight fell over the landscape, the stars shone
out so brightly in the clear blue canopy of the heavens
above, where bright Venus then beamed, shone alone as
the Queen of Light, amid the starry constellations and
clusters of golden jewels—she singing—

> " Star light,
>   Star bright,
>   The first star I have seen to-night ;
>   I wish I may,
>   I wish I might,
>   Have the wish I have wished to-night."

And so we rode on in a happy mood, repeating :

> " I see a star,
>   And the star sees me,—
>   And the star sees somebody
>   I would like to see."

It was another pearl of thought from the angel beside
me. Amid all this gush of joy and happiness, gross
darkness covered the land, and it was quite late in the
evening when we landed at the *summer* home of Per-
ham's mansion, on the common.

That evening there was a *German* at the hotel ; gallant soldiers moved under the enchantment of soft music,
and all went happily as a marriage-bell. Those who
know this dance, with all its rapturous and varied turns
and never-ending evolutions, will spare us the necessity
of further description. The next evening was beguiled
away by an exhibition of phantom shadows, under the
able direction of Professor Hernbrun, " with a display
of wonderful dentistry and tooth-drawing ;" with tight-
rope performance, not to be surpassed by even Blondin

himself, or Dr. Evans, of Paris, and only to be appreciated by those have been abroad and understand the mysteries of the German metaphysicians ; you may judge that there was plenty to amuse us while here. We had omitted to state that one of the most agreeable rides was that by the way of the East river and round through a thickly wooded bridle-path to Gooddell's farm, besides other drives to Chesterfield Lake, over Norcross Ferry, Slab Hollow, Broad Brook, and Leyden's Glen, and a point of view, the most interesting of all, at the extreme edge of the *Barracks*, where there can be seen one of the finest landscapes in or about the region of Brattleboro', on the line of the Connecticut river.

Thus ended our summer days at Stowe, and throughout the range of Vermont Hills there was nothing to mar the whole course of our journey. Any one who has been at Brattleboro' need not our measure of praise to herald its delights

The merits of Manchester are limited by her marble quarries and fine range of pasture land, the river Battenkill, and the Equinox Mountain. It is a very pleasant and a healthy village. But of all the places that we visited, our memories linger around the realms of Stowe. We heard of it before we became acquainted with its beauties ; the sound of the Indian name of its rivers, "The Winooski," or "The Wanouski," the Watumpsic, and its rapids, still lingers in our ears. The pleasant rides, the artist's dreamland, its noble mountain, its glens and notches, its boulder-rocks, its coy and hidden waterfalls, its scenery and picturesque valleys, and its inviting hostelry, which is a palace in its construction, affording comfort to its guests and its

seclusion, by ten miles or more from the line of any rail
road, render the village of Stowe worthy the name of
" The *Gem* of the Green Mountains," and we close with
this invitation, " *Go and see it*," and, if not satisfied,
settle down with this prescription of Murray, for your
comforter, in Italy. "*Vedi Napoli, e poi mori.*"

FOREIGN IMPUTATIONS.

In passing along Broadway numerous signs attract
your attention and you read the following : " Hotel kept
on the European Plan." When shall we get away from
this foreign influence which is daily absorbing the
virtue of the American character ? Why not, if we
must have foreign importations, do the best thing to be
done at once—that is to import the foreigner *in propria
persona*, and thereby get the whole benefit of this strange
animal, with his soul, strength, and spirit, so as to
swallow him whole ?

It is very evident that the ruin which has followed in
consequence of this national *caprice* needs no further
remark to confirm our statement ; and it is only by casting shadows that we can see these matters in a *new
light*, so as to remedy the evil.

The story of the reception of one of our missionaries
among the Sandwich Islands (where, by the way, the
true meaning of the word " *sandwich* " may be clearly
exhibited in the result of a queer miscegenation),
was narrated to a sea captain who had subsequently
visited those islands, after the death of the missionary.
The captain inquired of a *chief* whether he recoi-

lected an individual who had been sent out a few years previously, to christianize his subjects, and what he thought of the results of their pious endeavors." The chief hesitated a little to recall the identity of the gentleman alluded to, and, after shrugging his shoulders, with a humph, replied : " *Him me recollect ; him very goot man ; me eat him ; but him was werry tuff.*" Not very different is the handling of the foreign matter which is quietly introduced by our wily politicians to ingraft a new stock on the body politic, and who, after handling these subjects, come to grief over such an importation of foreign ingredients that they themselves are choked up by the gnats which they have swallowed, but have not strained under the burden of the *camels* which they had transported.

We ourselves are, and ever have been, American at heart. The United States are but a bundle of fagots bound together by a cord of union ; they will stand when all other nations perish. The union of hearts is the union of all the States, matrimonial or otherwise. If such financiers as Mr. Chase, Mr. Fessenden, and Mr. McCullough had been born and bred in England, they could not have devised any possible scheme by which to embarrass the wheels of commerce, American manufactures, and the farming interest of this country, so anti-republican, so anti-democratic as that abominable piece of treason by which they have sold us to the English bondholders, and thrust upon us a distracted gold currency, which has not even the *faculty* of running down hill, even after a shove from the Jews, the Shylocks, and the brokers on the Wall street corners.

"A WELCOME."

The soldier is home from the war,
Now returned from the battles afar;
Let us welcome the boys and the tar,
With our hip! hip! hip! and hurrah!

Fair Peace, like an angel, has spread
Her soft wings o'er the fields of the dead,
And, with hosts of archangels, rejoicing above,
Praise God, the Great Fountain of Love.

Let all hearts glow with gladness and pride,
While the Church doth rejoice as a bride;
O'er the plains where the war-horse has trod,
The foot-prints of Jesus stamp the image of God.

The fierce din of cannon no longer is heard,
Sweet violets are blooming near the low-bleating herd,
And the birds are now singing their song to the blest,
No longer affrighted from their soft, downy nests.

Where the red blood once sprinkled the face of the soil
These offsprings of martyrs have implanted their toil,
In the bosom of nature, in hopes of reward
From the Goddess of Liberty—a glorious award.

Thus ever in Providence, Faith and Repose
Are but blossoms of Virtue which blush as the rose.
And our broils are but thorns which through suffering arise,
That are pointed from Heaven to project to the skies.

ON SEEING A BOUQUET OF FLOWERS IN A GLASS VASE.

———

Sweet flowers! so like the smiles from heaven,
　To brighten all our hours of toil,
Wherefrom the reapers gather leaven,
　Resting whilom from mid-day broil.

How well they ease the burthened heart,
　Too often wet with briny tears,
Quite comforting: where all was smart,
　The pains which blight and sorrow rears.

How joyfully ye kiss the dews
　That bathe your soft and lovely skin.
While rainbow prisms vie in hues,
　To paint your glory, without stint.

Ye blooming children from the skies,
　Earth-born, yet bursting out in praise;
In grateful incense ye do rise,
　To honor love, and joy, and grace.

How gladly, then, we view these flowers,
　So snugly nestled in a vase of glass,
The fairest image of the passing hours,
　Too soon to break and fade away, alas!

THE DUAL TRIAD OF SISTERS.

There were three sisters, to my memory dear—
  Not long ago they lived across the river ;
These changed their names—not, I deem, from fear,
  But as the arrow's shot, when drawn from the quiver.

There are three others whom I chanced to know,
  Among the Graces of this modern city,
Who have not merely spent their lives for show,
  So modest are they, but keen to claims for pity.

The first of these, not rated as a beauty,
  But well disposed toward the meek and poor,
Always contented to perform her duty,
  Nor to the homeless ever shuts her door.

Unselfish, wise, and ever well intended,
  Her heart inclines her well to answer every call ;
No beggar ever quits her empty-handed—
  E'en were she once in quest of gayety and ball.

The second, beauty had—a form like Venus,
  In height the Medici, figure lithe and light ;
Well versed in poetry and every art amœnous,
  And with a spirit which yields us all delight.

The third, brunette, a connoisseur and good,
  Gifted in drawing from the life and cast—
Has a sweet friend who boasts of Indian blood;
  Both, in their studio, glory in the past.

Despite the difference in their various style,
  Their very contrasts lead to happy unity ;
Thus beauty, use, and taste beguile
  Their hours, well spent in love and holy unity.

The dual three are here Earth's witnesses of Heaven,
  The double manifest of the blessed Trinity :
Faith, Hope, and Charity, with Love, are leaven—
  God, and His Son, and Holy Spirit are Divinity.

MORAL.
The happy dual of the married state is perfect Love—
  And not less blessed when the heart is single ;
The Spirit, water, and the blood are shadows from above,
  And where Christ's Spirit dwells, heaven and earth
    commingle.

THE TOMB OF THE MARTYRS.

What hallowed associations are connected with the sound of martyrdom ! The heart of the patriot, the lover of his country, the true American, the honest man, and the sincere Christian, swells with emotions too deep for utterance. Great thoughts of heart arise in the bosom of all brave men, and noble women weep over the memories of the sacred dead :

"Dulce et decore est pro patriâ mori."

Adjoining the United States Navy Yard in Brooklyn city, in Jackson street, may be seen, in a dilapidated condition, the tomb of the martyrs who died in dungeons and pestilential prison-ships, in and about the city of New York, during the seven years of our Revolutionary War.

What a disgrace to their living descendants, that the only monument that was ever erected to their memory should be suffered to remain in the sad and sorry plight in which it appears to-day !

It is high time that Brooklyn should wake up to a proper sense of their neglect of these departed worthies, and take the matter in hand, and rear a monument in some conspicuous spot, worthy of themselves, and which the children of future generations might visit, in order to keep alive and fresh their pride and honor for such patriotic exemplars. It would be a grand idea to mingle the bones of these heroes of the Revolution with those of the illustrious dead who have lately fought, bled, and died in our recent conflict against this last devilish Rebellion. Where rests your sense of shame, ye incorporators of Kings? Why have these ashes of your patriotic ancestors to be sanctified only by the colonists of New England; and why should the sapient wisdom of New Connecticut be called upon alone to place a statue over the buried martyrs in their vault and mouldering coffins at the purlieus of Wallabout? Why leave it to old Benjamin Romaine solely, as a monnment to his undying love and patriotism, and utter detestation of English impudence, to devise his body to the lot, in which these patriots have to inherit only their own bones, or to crown his pure devotion in a coronet of glory, which only exhibits thereon dark shadows in a strong contrast to the grim indifference of these Moabites of Long Island? Let the government lay hold of this matter, and sink their disgrace in a noble tribute to the memory of these glorious ancestors of our Independence! If they fail to do their duty, let us of Manhattan shame our neighbors on the other side of the East river into the doing of the correct thing in the present necessity. If these fail, let the spirit of the old Constitution itself, " that undying and perpetual charter of human rights, and of our duties to God and man," rise up like the bones of Elisha, which stood up on their feet at the indignant outrage of that band of wandering invaders, who, while casting only a very common man's corpse into the sepulchre of this venerable saint and prophet of old, plead that the dry bones of these modern vandals might shake in frightful

apprehension of that irrepressible disgrace and contumely with which posterity will visit them for their
shameful neglect, and their remissful memories of the
past heroes of the Revolution, when it comes their turn
to be buried in vaults, and their ashes to be blown to
the winds in a tempest of tornadoes and tea-table talk
and reproach. Verily, the ashes of those dead patriots
are the embryo of the resurrection of our country ; and
we cannot better consecrate the ground where these
martyrs of the dust are buried so well as by raising
altars in the present on which the living may offer such
a savor of sweet incense as shall yield that consolation
and comfort of holy sacrifice, of thanksgiving, glory, and
praise, to heal the broken hearts of the widows and the
orphans, whose sorrows and wounds would be only
freshly opened, but for the recollection that the heroes
of the Revolution, and the honorable dead, brought forth
upon this *continent* a new nation, which was conceived
for the enjoyment of a greater liberty for all mankind,
which shall survive the wreck of empire and the fall of
kings, and shall endure only so long as we who are
alive shall honor their memories within the land which
the Lord our God has given us: It is but meet that we
dedicate a portion of our soil as the final resting-place
of those who gave their lives that this nation might live
forever. *" Requiescant in pace."*   Let us fi" up the
measure of their devotion.   Amen.

A REFRAIN.

I hope
I have not lost thee, Mary,
 I'm only thrust one side.
I had no prurient fantasy
 To sue thee as my bride.

'Twas a spirit that misled me,
 As thou knelt in silent prayer,
That an angel had descended
 Through the dim, religious air.

I was thinking of that Mary
 Whom Jesus loved as friend,
When sister Martha was so gary,
 And wouldn't stay to mend.

Thy dreamy gaze involved me,
 As I was passing down the aisle,
And its magic so dissolved me,
 That it made St. Cle . . smile.

On a raining Sunday morning,
 As I sauntered in to prayers,
A messenger in sackcloth, mourning,
 Whispered slily in my ears:

"Would you like to know Miss Leamey?
 "Faith," says I, "I dinna care."
It rather made me dreamy
 With my usual debonaire.

Then reflecting on the matter;
 For she looked so very sweet;
How the deuce was I to get at her,
 And contrive how we might meet.

Thus tempted with heard praises
Of her arts and skill in look—
For you know I love the Graces—
I discharged at her a book;

That was penned by Mistress Adams.
Not she for poor Adam's ail,
The father of all those little damms
That have made our race so pale—

Which, projected at my lassie,
The subject of these verses,
Came back like coach, with glasses,
Which follows solemn hearses.

I'm right sorry for the authoress,
I thought only for her good—
Case did not suit the doctoress;
She needed better food.

But spring came on with its verdure,
With its shining coat of green,
And Astarte sent some flowers,
The rarest to be seen.

And the patient had recovered
From the offerings and the book,
But relapses were discovered,
And of a serious turn partook.

'Twas an admiration offering only;
What's the harm in such a thing?—
When the subject is a lady,
And cat may look at king.

MORAL:

"Drink water out of your own cisterns and running water out
of your own wells."
"Cast thy bread upon the waters, and it shall return to thee
after many days."

BLOOMINGDALE STAGE MEMORIES.

Friend, hast thon ever been at Bloomingdale?
And ridden in the Stages which ran in time of Moore,
And split your side in such a boisterous gale,
That you did cry, because you could laugh no more.

Now, since that, from the days of Lntz & Doll to this,
Have Babies filled the Baskets held by simple Nurses;
There's been no change towards bettering human bliss,
Although one Churchill runs the Stage o'er hillside or by
Churches.

E'er first appeared Baby, a Basket foretold its ominous presence;
Only to type the Cradle by which it was to be rocked asleep,
And when Mam Dobson weighed the little dear omnipotence,
'Twas but the balance of the first stage from which it was to
peep.

And ever since times of Adam, when Baby took his ticket of
Leave,
There's been no respite from the various modes of travel,
The Man or Woman, Boy or Girl, have had no sure reprieve,
Whether the road they cabbed o'er was dirt road, sand, or
gravel.

The History of Manhattan hath a page so ample, that no book
Of Travel ever shook the sides of any passenger through life,
As the encounters in that horrible stage, we follow sufferers took,
Where we were fumbled, jumbled, tumbled, as if 'twere in
battle strife.

Now we all remember Father Hardinge, with his huge cravat
so high,
Through which he shook his horse-laugh until he made us
snicker;
And how Jane Tompson grumbled, as the children set up their
cry,
The rumbling wagon groaned more shaky, and the clouds of
dust grew thicker.

'Tis ever thus from childhood's hour, all our lives we are
dragged along,
E'en from the day the infant left the arms of puling nurse,
Up to the day when old age sighs and weeps o'er days long gone,
Until the last sad hour when "*Mors est Omnibus*" changes
into Hearse.

A RAMBLE IN JULY,

A lady and a lassie and a lad,
  On a smiling July day,
Stepped out of the cars into Central Park,
  There happily to spend the day.

It was the first time in his life
  That the lad had seen the Ramble,
For he was led there like a little sheep,
  That had only just learned to gambol.

And ever as from little things a lesson we may learn,
  And from a small spark a great big fire may rise,
So it often seems that as troubled heart may burn,
  Should mortal from sepulchral earth be lifted to the skies.

Now we will change the age of him we called the lad,
  For men are but children first, but babes in later days,
And speaking boldly say 'twas a young man, be gad!
  Who was the first sad subject of these sorry lays.

It matters not even if a Red Rose of Lancaster
  Went with our party, she of maturer age,
As if one Pollox strayed away with Castor,
  'Twas all the worse for this little gentle page.

Nor makes it better that a white Rose of York,
  So sweetly smiled upon this youth forlorn,
For what's a smelling-bottle without its cork,
  Or what avails a valley without ripened corn?

Secundo, we will change the nature of our metre—
  The day itself was changeable, as all fine weather is—
To ask the Muse to try a new gasometer,
  To let our gas off with a double whiz.

On a bright summer morning in the middle of July, the day
  As I was passing o'er the road, 'twas the 20th of July.
The sun was flirting with the clouds like hide-and-seek in play,
  When whom did I chance to meet but the idol of my eye.

'Twas very naughty of me, as you may well suppose,
  That such a man of business should be stopping by the way,
To cull a sweet white lily that was nestled near a Rose,
  Or to spend an hour by the fountain as it was dallying in its
    play.

The little golden diamonds that it scattered in the light
  Spread in starry shadows as it sparkled to the sun,
And my happy thoughts like violets bursting the night
  Of nursing mother earth, so inspired me I could not run.

We know the golden hours which were running like a stream,
  Though speut in sweet communion would ne'er return again
But the fountain and the flowers were weaving a sweet theme,
  Had been painted by the angels on Nature's wide domain.

It was of a stolen flower, that was pitcher-like in form,
  As it floated from its pendant, very like an ear-ring,
That one would have hardly thought of any harm,
  Or that there was aught of wrong in such a little thing.

But there ever was in stolen fruit a deal of mischief lurking,
  Even as where, in old Romaint, a maiden was stolen away
From her father's castellated halls, when gallant knight went
    barking
  And casting but a cloak around her, in his bark sped through
    the spray.

There never was since time of Eve, when Adam was away,
  But some de'il was there, to whisper slyly in the ear
There's something good in stealing, not, but there's the devil to
    pay,
  And no harm that any ill will happen then to fear.

3

Now what shall be said when in another older saying
You read that one cannot teach an old dog new tricks,
For even the elder lady pulled a sprig of jessamine, laying
Not far from where a party sat on a bench of rustic sticks.

"'Twas ever thus, from childhood's hour,
I've seen my fondest hopes decay ;
I never loved a tree or flower,
But 'twas the first to fade away.

"—Tom Moore."

Another poet, not so well read in verse,
Doth now conclude this model prosaidy
By, never do write from railroad car, nor disperse
Your thoughts from office calls—even for a lady.

—

MORAL.

Old Benjamin Franklin, so wise in his days,
Was given to verses, but never to lays—
'Twere a pity the moderns don't mind what he says,
If they did, 'twould be surely more to their praise.

Take care of the shop, and the shop will care for you ;
Always button your coat, and fasten your shoes,
And then some fair lady will seek for a friend
Who'll be true with her lover to life's bitter end.

COLONEL O'BRIAN;

OR,

THE SOLDIER OF FORTUNE.

BY ONE WHO KNEW HIM.

Seize upon truth where'er 'tis found;
Among your friends, among your foes,
On Christian or on heathen ground;
The flower 's divine where'er it grows;
Refuse the prickle and assume the rose.

Fitz O'Brian, of Irish descent, was a soldier of fortune, who, during the wars on the Spanish main, was engaged by the South Americans in waging war against the rebels of that country. Noble, generous, and brave, with a courage as indomitable as the lion, without fear and without reproach, he endeared himself to our countrymen, because he was a patriot and a true friend of all inclined to universal liberty.

He led the armies of the noble republics of that southern land or continent, overcame the enemies of the government, and after a successful campaign, which ended in putting all the revolutionists to flight, laid down his arms to settle down in glorious peace.

The government would have covered him with all the honors due to such braves, and they did indeed invest him with those paltry trinkets of gilt medals, and the flaming insignia of titles covered him with an emblazonry of gold lace, but could not hide his merit or his

virtues. He refused all compensation for his services,
and spent all his patrimony of English gold freely as
water, or as his own caprices suited. He was a gallant,
bold, reckless, and chivalrous man. Like Don Quixote,
he fought for the love of it. The gayest of soldiers, a
true-hearted, rollicking, rioting, frolicking Irishman,
and as true to his honor as the dial to the sun.

I knew him well. I loved his hearty, free, rough-and-
ready manner. There was a sparkle in his eyes and
sunshine in his laughter. He displayed his fun at all
times, and was as eccentric as he was bold, and gifted as
he was gay.

Among his prospects, for he was somewhat of a specu-
lative character, was his interest in a valuable silver
mine, hid in the heart of the Andes, or it matters not
where—say some part of Peru. This he offered to a
friend for the privilege of working it, simply on the condition that he should pay all his debts, amounting to
only about $15,000, a mere trifle, and a cheap bargain
for a mine which has yielded over $5,000,000 per an-
num.

The only risk attending the purchase would be, perhaps, the loss of the man's head who attempted to de-
velop its treasures, and the fact that there needed a
great deal of pumping before the water could be drawn
out, which had been overflowing the adits for a number
of years back.

The history of this mine was rather singular. One
Zalmanezer, a clever old Indian, had once been the
owner of this property. It had been a gift from the
empire for the many valuable services he had performed,
but it was taken from him by one of those peculiar *coups*

d'états so common to despots, and concealed under the
name of diplomatic tact, which sometimes compensates
their most faithful servants by cutting off their heads.
The influence of this aboriginal was so great among his
native subjects that the government became jealous of
him, and after having first baited him with the offer of a
fee simple of this his paramount estate of inheritance,
accused him of tampering with the privities of royalty
and the king's domains ; and although he proffered a
thousand dollars a day whilst he waited his answer to
an appeal to the parent government of Spain, they
refused his bail against the act by dishonorable and
treacherous conduct on their part at home, who conclud-
ed that the best mode of getting rid of the popularity
of this subject was to cut off his head, and thus control
the entire right of possession.

Thus ever republics show their ingratitude. This is
a solemn proverb and a warning, and, like the farmer
and his goose, they killed the bird in order to get her
eggs. To remedy the short-sightedness exhibited in this
picture of ingratitude, the companions of the Indian and
his bosom friends, grateful and reminiscent of his many
friendly acts among the neighbors, very ingeniously con-
trived to pull out the plugs that had stopped the little
streams usually gushing out of the cavities in all mines
through the crevices, and obstructing the proper working of the laborers, and thus letting in a flood of water,
burst the sources of the neighboring lake, and thereby
destroyed the schemes of the avaricious governor of
Peru, and thus placed a barrier to all future attempts to
get this silver. Thus Providence interrupts the course
of human monsters, and by a certain retribution puts a

stop to the evil as the beginning complot. Truly, "man proposes, but God disposes." "Vengeance is mine," saith the Lord. The poor Indian has become a constellation of silver—in heaven—by way of compensation.

But to return to our friend the Colonel. He had various talents beside those of soldiering and gallant offices. Not unskillful was he in the magic art of legerdemain, and he often, among his circle of friends at the old "*stone arm-chair*," where he had built an adobe palace, showed them his tricks of sleight-of-hand, which he had learned, while a youth, at "Donnybrook Fair." Here at this altar of festive repose he drank many a bumper, and amid the sparkle of the wine and the brighter flashes of his wit our rollicking, frolicking, and happy Hibernian became green as the lizards of the Old Erin Island whilst he rejoiced in his cups. This art was learned when he was poor, at home, and went to the fair to sharpen his wits for something to spend, like Curran, his countryman, to whistle away the hunger. Thus he lived, and after having frolicked and feasted, fought and played, he returned to the old country after having fought an arrant English officer, who had squinted too hard at one of his friend's sweethearts on board a man-of-war, in the offing, near Rio Janeiro.

The last we hear of him was after his return to Ireland, where he had expected to end his days. And in a racy letter to one of his early friends on the main he writes : " We have been up to the Lakes of Killarney, and it was nothing but swimming and hunting, hock and champagne."

OLD RELICS OF '76.

———

Hast thou ever been at *Deacon*'s,
    He who lives on Harlem Lane,
The host that strengthens weak ones,
    And gives them physic for their pain ?

For preamble to my story, 'tis well for us to explain,
There are physics for the body, and also for the soul ;
There are pills that very complex are, and others very plain,
Some taken in a roll of bread, and sometimes in a bowl.

There are tricks in every calling, but certes, none in ours,
For the doctors, as well as lawers, must all a living make,
Scarce would we except the Clergy, who so well exert their
      powers,
For other people's ailings, and metaphysics take.

There are Canon's in the Church, and nippers in the shop,
As well as keys of skeleton shape, which rusty safes unlock,
But the wonders of that magic key, which is taken in a drop,
Hath a power which overshadows human reason in the shock.

Fain would we run a tilt against the force of human reason,
Fight the Doctors of Divinity, or Medicine, or Law,
Lest some orator from pulpit, or smart counselor, in treason,
Might upset us by his logic, and crack us in the jaw.

What boots this rhodomontade, that's so very far from point ?
If the same were too protracted, 'twould take us off our track
From the place from which we started, and put all out of
      joint,—
So 'tis best to turn our Pegasus, and lead him a little back.

There was a dreadful sound of cannons when the Spirit of
    Seventy-six
Roused the patriots of Long Island, to arrest that bloody band
Of Hessians and Red-coats, with their frightful bayonets fixed,
Who had landed on our native soil, from their poor old foreign
    land.

The heart of every patriot was fired, to a man,
And the women even started to lend a helping hand,
As the horrid foe advanced up the narrow pass McGowan,
And the thundering boom of English guns sounded wildly o'er
    the strand.

'Twas just where our noble WASHINGTON, well mounted on his
    steed,
Dashed down upon these rebels, to check their fierce advance,
And our gallant little army, raised up in time of need,
Sent these rascals to the Devil in a very hasty dance.

It was in sight of Harlem heights, quite near the Magazine,
Which still is sighted where Central Park is walled in,
And these relics of our story were taken from their screen,
Where they had long been buried deep, some fifteen feet within.

'Twas very natural for the Deacon, who dwells at Avenue Six,
To be careful of these relics from that famous battle line,
And to furnish up these heavings from landslide in a new fix,
To keep alive our Father's memory, and for auld lang syne.

'Tis not true, as Deacon's daughters are exhibited to fame,
With all the sons of ministers, as of a very streaky kind,
But the conversion is quite proper, by all our men of name,
That our ancestors were gallant men, and never found behind.

Oft as we read in ancient history, that Herodotus was blind
To the sacred deeds of heroes, who had freely shed their blood;
But to modern it is left to speak a word more kind
For all our gallant heroes, and of the buried dead, nothing else
    but good.

And as we viewed these solemn relics at the inn at Harlem Lane,
The cannon ball so rusty, and the key and nippers square,
It struck us most profoundly, that the hostlers at that fane
Must have shod enormous horses, or that iron was very rare.

And the further we reflected, as we stopped to drink within,
That the successor of these ancients were not so far ahead
Of the worthies of last century, in their fondness for poor gin,
Although the Dutch of our days drink lager by the hogshead.

MORAL.

Now the substance of our present poem hath its finale in a verse,
That we are actors all in tragedy, and comedy, and crime,
And that our men and women, from the cradle to the hearse,
Are but types of the poor Prodigal, but not Nazarites of time.

3*

A PSALM OF LIFE.

———

"There is a river, the streams whereof make glad the city of God
—*Psalm* xlvi., 4.

———

Thus sang the Psalmist in the olden time,
To whom God lent grace to put his verse in rhyme;
When poet sanctified for praise and song,
Gave glory to their Lord, the whole day long.

And as the birds sing at the morning hours,
Raising sweet melodies aloft with all their powers,
So did the son of Jesse lift his voice in praise,
And tuned his harp's string for eternal lays.

So not unlike the river, whose streams make glad
The cities by whose walls the rapid current gleams,
And prospects furnish for those golden dreams
Wherein the poets raved and Troubadours grew sad.

Walking by side of flowing streams, the fishes gamboling t
      delight,
And gayly sporting, appear to disappear as in a dream,
And green twigs bending, bow to their ruling might,
While drooping willows bend in homage to the stream.

What are the rivers flowing but the means of grace
God's living image stamped on Nature's pleasing face;
The blood of Jesus and the Holy Spirit seem
The only life upon the bosom of the silent stream.

The lovely prospects which, by faith, are throwing
Their shadows from the substance of angelic forms,
Signs are of springs, those welling fountains showing
The great eternal source of vernal morns.

The traffic which the soul herself doth carry on
Is but the business of the far-off main,
And all the merchandise that is brought thereon
Is but the harvesting of the golden grain.

Product of silver, and all alloy of gold refined,
Which by the Cross is purified and cleared,
Do but engrave the image of the workman's mind,
And stamp reflections from His likeness reared.

And where no water was, in dry and barren field,
What happiness burst forth from out the hidden sand,
And gushing springs from grassy meadows yield
Gardens well watered by Jehovah's hand.

What rich supplies where all other resource fails,
And all have access to the God of grace;
How free the franchise from old Satan's jails,
When found security in the Saviour's face. *

These are the means which satisfy the soul—
Our Saviour's blood, the living bread from heaven,
The Spirit's influence, the body's just control,
The Gospels freely spread, that holy leaven.

Which from the incense of our hearts are sent
Up to the courts of heaven, in humble sacrifice,
And lift our souls upward in meek ascent,
Where love shall wipe all tears from mortal eyes.

Then will the Cross be softened, and head be fit for crown,
Here crucified in sorrow, there will true joy be found,
When Jacob's ladder will once more be lifted down,
And heaven found here, where all is holy ground.

And if such sweetness here be drop'd in earthly streams,
Where sins are pardoned, if by faith our eyes we raise,
What must that fountain be in those blessed realms,
Where saints and angels draw their bliss from praise;

Where God himself shall see us face to face,
And Jesus stamps His heirship with His seal of love;
Where happy seraphs, clad in white, their robes of grace,
Shall tune their harps, and sing aloud, above.

Then, brothers, help us—refresh our thirst for glory,
Seek for thy Saviour, full of grace and truth,
Trust Him with all thy heart, believe this simple story,
And keep such childlike faith as that of gentle Ruth.

TRIADS OF THE PAST AND PRESENT.

There were three brothers, in the old times of Rome,
· Who from their mother's fireside were sent to travel ;
And o'er the earth were strongly bent to roam,
    While all the rest of us were forced to stay at home and
      grabble.

As all men are naturally savage in their nature,
    And from the earth spring forth by human birth,
'Tis not so strange that every mortal creature
    Should, before death, be taxed to eat his peck of earth.

And as in every soil there is always found some gravel,
    And mother-earth is burthened for her share;
For all creation groaneth under heavy travail,
    No wonder that her bowels should be opened with a plow·
      share.

And as men grown up collect themselves in rabbles,
    There's some confusion happens in selection of fit wives ;
Thus, out of mixed ideals, oft spring up family quarrels,
    While how to find a proper helpmate is the puzzle of their
      lives.

So when the Sabines settled in the neighborhood of Rome,
    They were living very quietly until Romulus appeared ;
He who killed his brother Remus for running of his wall down.
    'Twas but the wolf in nature, under whose nursing he was
      reared.

Thus ever speaks all history, that tells of sorry fight,
    That the weak one against the mighty had not a right at all,
That a light antagonist had no counting on his weight,
    And in the conqueror's victory the only glory is in his fall.

And as in every evil that has happened under the sun,
There's a woman at the bottom of the gravamen of trouble,
Who coolly views these matters as a pretty piece of fun,
And weighs the issue of the combat as a child would blow a
    bubble.

Thus, when the Romans became tired of a lonely single life,
They pitched into the Sabines, in a kind of mixed raid,
And each shouldering a burthen in the shape of a young wife,
Left behind, by way of comforter, only the handle of the blade

But as to every human grief, there's a way for consolation,
For the Sabine fathers ever entertained his country's good a
    heart,
In that there might some good arise from this queer miscegena-
    tion,
And that it were better to live together than to live and figh:
    apart.

So another case of satisfaction took place in similar cause,
When the Horatii and Curatii got into a shameful scrape,
And the women rushed in to rescue in the midst of their angry
    jaws,
And thus saved these ancient pugilists a vast expense for crape.

This is but a clear illustration of that diplomatic dress
Which covers up the skeleton that is said to be hid in every
    house,
When a woman, with her tact and subtle, sly address,
Slips in between the combatants, to make it still as a mouse

Abosh now to ancient history, and all these valorous Three,
We moderns have progressed beyond, and war's now turned
    to peace,
And we are pleased to tell another tale in this land now clear and
    free,
Of a certain happy triple band, whose friendship brings me
    ease.

These are living on a quiet street, where the corner never meets,
  Where are passages and alleyways, not far from Freres across
    the way,
But no passenger intrudes here, and no sister sly leer greets
  Nor salutation from a stranger, by, "Sir, are you going to the
    play?"

But this union of brothers whom I am bound to call my friends
  Having such a charming sweet variety of little airs and graces.
That all the banterings of repartee and sharp difference of ends
  Would not change a single feature of their noble, handsome
    faces.

Talk of parts and cultivation, the Romans and the Greeks
  Could not hold a candle for the varied lights that shine
Through the windows of their intellects which every wisdom
    seeks,
  To illuminate the windows of this crazy bark of mine.

The first, he, of Paganini, took a notion to procure
  All the old Cremonas he could get from every southern sea
    remote, .
And once listen as he soundeth his Barbiton so sure,
  You'd thought that all Eolia had sent his winds afloat.

That even Melebeus to his Tityrus couldn't warble songs so pure
  That even the sweet nightingale singing out her songs at night
In the vales of Valambrosa, where the herbs are sure to cure,
  And woods are filled with fragrance that yields the soul
    delight.

With a brother not so gifted, but remarkable in mind and cul-
    tivation,
  Who would not exchange his native home for any foreign
    place,
In any court of Europe, surely not for France, that very funny
    nation,
  Where Americans are sadly noted for their fondness of
    grimace.

There still remains another scion of this family of R maine,
Whose ancestry from Scottish chiefs had an offshoot very old
They were canny as old cavaliers of the brightest days of Spain,
Who were clever at the short-sword and habergeon, and bold,

As the lions of Castile or the braves of Salamanca,
And bright as the sun at Port-del-Sol near by the rough
Sierras bold,
Which frown in all that keenest cold, over the vales of poor
La Mancha,
Where the old hidalgoes gossip, and merchandise is sold.

The last, he was a counselor-at-law, and of that very clever wit,
Which could rightly guide the ship of State through many a
blowing storm,
Who, as to his churchmanship, was the equal of Dewitt,
So gifted was he in canon lore, and every rubric form.

Thus with music and with chivalry, and every other grace united,
These brothers were like preux Bayards in this very pleasant
family,
Blessed with the virtues of their parents, who were so good and
holy plighted;
For had their lives been fully read, 'twould seem like ancient
homily.

Such as when one finds in the archives of the old convents
samples,   .
Where illuminated missals decked in every form of fruits and
flowers,
Blooming entwined 'mid angels in a marginal of beautiful
examples.
Just as the holy monks passed all their lives in prayer and
happy hours.

NEWTOWN, BUT NOT NEWTONIAN.

" A SERIOUS TALE."

It is an old proverb that "when rogues fall out, honest men get their rights." Lord Bacon very quaintly has remarked, in that clever style of philosophy which formed the origin of the inductive school, that " he is the best man who does the best thing to be done in the times in which he is living."

But modern philosophers have rather reversed the practical teachings of induction, and being led astray by certain foolish schemes of their own invention, and governed always by that supreme autocracy of self, which brooks no rival and courts no counsel, having once departed from that great charter of all human rights, " By the sweat of your brow you shall earn your bread," very fanatically getting something on the brain, make fearful leaps into gulfs that know no bottom, and, like ships without ballast, flounder into a perplexity of difficulties and danger, as horrible as the maelstrom, and as deep as the grave. Such have always been swallowed up by their own vanity, and have gone to the very bottom of the oozy deep.

Hardly any of those philosophers who planted the Utopia of Newtown ever sat down to consider that all *Chateaux en Espagne* have been ever built upon bladders and balloons, typically illustrating those genera of animated nature denominated as looms and balloons. But we pass over such infirmities of the human species, and proceed at once to the moral, which will close up this chapter in our annals of Foolishness.

A forlorn maiden who had once lost a husband, thrown upon the world for a support to be derived from those friends whom she had known during the lifetime of her better half, in the depth of her grief and sorrow fled into the wilderness of misfortune to conceal her meditations and her misery ; alas ! she found with the poet that—

> " When lovely woman stoops to folly,
>   And finds, alas ! that men betray,
> What grief can soothe her melancholy,
> What tears can wash her grief away ?"

Guilty in the sense of having swallowed a gilded pill, she found out too late that it was but a poisoned chalice.

We have no particular enmity against any class of lunatics. Many have been confined as such who were merely simpletons. A more dangerous class have been left out of the mad-house to prey upon the world at large, who, having no feelings for humanity as the sad, earnest, but weak creations of a beneficent Providence, draw large drafts on their imagination for their facts ; and by their own blindness, curtailed of the first elementary properties of good sense, like the fox in the fable, with his tail cut off, wish to draw the rest of mankind into the fashion of wearing no tails at all. We mourn not the tales of that celebrated authoress, "whose tales were so severely lashed by the critics that they continue still to be read to this day." The friends of the community at Newtown have, ever since the bursting of their bubble, been so red from a sorry sense of shame that they never like to hear of their follies in the past, when they were garrisoned in that charnel-house of diseased brains, and were fed on mash marrow, which they dipped out with a general spoon.

How like spoonies they have since felt at the least reminder of such ephemeral fantasies ; and how like jackanapes they have since appeared to each other when thinking of the tales of their common washtubs, alongside of the machinery bread knives, common potatoes, fixings, and philosophical pea-pod shellings, with lunatical rhapsodies over the large tin basin ?

Verily the gods with hyperion curls and ambrosial locks seemed again to have left Olympus, and Pan himself ruled over sheep and shepherdesses in these Arcadian groves.

How sweet the potatoes tasted under the soothing melody of fostering music ! How did the groves resound with the nasal blasts of Arcadian jackasses ! Italian nightingales were but blackbirds or crows to these. The very pillars in their temple in the groves were fragrant with soft incense, and delicious perfumes breathed through the openings of the porticoes. The savory smell of common mortals' dinners was too Hibernian for these new lights of the world. Humanitarianism shut up its nose at the very mention of broad acres and the practical cultivation of the soil.

Farming was to be carried on by simple speculations on the theory of development, and pork and beans were to be *exorcised* into winds from old Boreas, and vegetation was to sprout by spontaneous combustion into the esthetical elements of a supernatural philosophy and superhuman contrivances for dispensing with the use of labor.

Children were to be raised by the easy process of inoculating them with those blocks of beauties that were presented to their gloating visions. Photographic reflections of sunlight were to paint the beauty of all existences into the very soul of the embryo infant. The parent was to conceive only to beget a perfect child, and all the natural devil which might have been transmitted to the child by some unfortunate ancestor was to be driven out by the bare depiction of a winged seraph planted on the branches of a blossoming peach-tree.

Humanity was thus buried in the apocalypse of earth, and all nature was shrouded for a cataplasm of entombment, so gorgeous, so brilliant, glorious, and inviting that perfection was to be established as a mere matter of course, and the beatitudes were to bloom in the bosom of godliness, and repose there in a symposium of Apollonic forms and sympathetic graces, where all the gardens were to breathe of the otto of roses, and the sky of the soul was to be that interior life of virtue which was too delicate to be bruised, and not unlike the atmosphere preponderating man not felt by these puling pollywogs and modern Abderites.

The disciples of old Zoroaster were far behind these modern sky-scrapers, who were for sweeping the moon before they had purchased a ladder to reach it ; and not unlike those philosophers, of like wisdom, these were building fountains where there was no water to fill them, and statues raised so high in the air that the images could hardly be seen by the skylark

Such men as these want no Sunday to rest in ; wiser

than Providence, they often forget to procure any pro-
vender to fill their hollow bodies. Having gas-light in
their heads, they carry lanterns inside of earthen pitch-
ers, which, being struck with implements, like spiritual
violins, give out uncertain sounds, and yield no harmo-
nics, but very sorry groanings. Like voltaic batteries,
constructed of copper and zinc, they have a large share
of brass, and are dead to any sensibilities for communi-
cations to human intelligences. They build up mansions
in the overland to inhabit them, as they sink in the
northern seas, and their reflections, like the flashes of
the *aurora*, are as evanescent as the bubbles from the
bottom of a river, and luminously flashing and lurid as
the phosphorescent emissions from rotten punk. Such
people, not unlike empty vessels when struck, always
sound the loudest.

FINALE.

GARDENS OF DELIGHT.

"While within my garden roving,
    And my senses all aro fed,
Rising from these loved attractions,
    I'm to nobler subjects led.
        Other gardens
    Here, in musing, oft I tread.

"In the Church, the *Saviour's* garden,
    Trees and plants and flowers I see;
Guarded, watered, trained, and cherished,
    Blooming immortality;
        All, O Calvary!
    All derived *alone* from thee.

"But, above all gardens precious,
    See the *heavenly* Paradise;
There the Tree of Life is bearing;
    There the springs of glory rise:
        And the richness
    Every want supplies.

"There the foot no thorn e'er pierces;
    There the heart ne'er heaves a sigh;
There in white we walk with *Jesus*,
    All our loved connections by.
        And to reach it
    'Tis a privilege to die."

—JAY.

FINIS.

INDEX.

SING SING,

OR

PRISON LIFE.

—

Ugly indorsements of the puzzle and perplexity of
society, hateful fruits of a tree whose roots trip us in
every court and alley, baleful apples of Hesperus,
guarded by a dragon with leather spectacles over his
hundred eyes, are our prisons, for how many among us
really know anything of them? Gradgrind has statis-
tics, plenty of them; he is learned in police reports,
posted in the matter of contracts. Easy people in
general are put off by the dictionary. Careless people
visit them very much as they would a menagerie, without so much as a guess at this world as sad, as silent,
as intimately interwoven with all our living and doing,
and almost as unknown as the kingdom of lost spirits.
But try now a little to conceive what this life really is—
a life that commences with a rattling of bolts and jarring
of heavy iron doors, a going over of registers, and a
shuffling tramp along the stony wards of men and
women going to their work; rules differing somewhat
in the various institutions, associations allowed in
some, solitary meals and work required in others, but
everywhere life parceled, measured out; women stitch-
ing in silence, men moving about amidst creaking,
grinding, clicking, hammering, all manner of uncouth
machine noises, impressive as statues, forlorn as Eblis,
but all working with a horrible automaton-like indus-
try; wax-like neatness (for government is the best of
housekeepers), system, precision, order, vigilance
everywhere.

This is the surface ice. Kid-glove finger-tip philanthropy is powerless to break it. Far-off preaching
from the heights of our virtue is too cool to melt it. To

know anything of these Hecla hearts, there must be an actual going down among the publicans and sinners. We must at least allow these felons the common ground of our humanity; must picture to ourselves this humanity in most instances possessed of a childhood without hope or memory of tenderness, without knowledge of the name of God, much less His nature, with no teacher but instinct, no incentive but want, arriving at maturity with no resources but those of sin, no creed but that of the devil ; those who have fallen from at least an outward respectability, pressed down with shame, maddened with regret and anxiety, and filled with horror at the vile companionship into which they are thrown. Such are the flock of black sheep whom we must either lead or drive. Let them alone we cannot, it being one of the pleasant peculiarities of sin that, if we do not find it out, it will us, coming up into our very bed-chambers with the impudence of the frogs of Egypt.

Decision between the two systems (leading and driving) seems easy, if success be admitted as a test of merit, yet on no subject is there louder or more unsatisfactory debate. It is fiercely argued :

"You must whip and starve your menagerie into submission. Put down the rebellious beasts as Alderman Cute did young mothers and suicides, and keep them down."

It is keenly contended in reply:

"If, after you have chained and whipped your tiger for the given term of years, he still shows no leaning to the lamb persuasion, might it not be wiser to let loose a menagerie of the four-footed striped gentry than one striped biped, lower in degradation, blacker in purpose, harder in heart than when the relentless gates first closed upon him ?" Meanwhile an officer twenty-three years in the service, in an interesting work (Life in Sing Sing), offers a little of the much needed light on the different theories, and their operation.

Solitary confinement without labor had been tried at Auburn, with such success that, out of eighty convicts thus immured, five died, one went raving mad, one poor soul watched his time and dashed himself over the gallery, and government was fain to let loose the rest in all haste lest it should be found guilty of murder within the year. In 1839 an uneasy public conscience spoke out in the report of a Prison Committee, a radical document, boldly affirming "that convicts were influenced by hopes and fears, capable of reflection and judgment, moved to anger by stripes, governed, like the rest of mankind, by their mental faculties." This Jacobin of a Committee takes exception to punishments of eighty or a hundred lashes, inflicted by an instrument which multiplies every stroke by six for small offenses. One thousand lashes in three weeks for a maniac convict, were pronounced too many. Moral burying alive, by prohibition of all letters, visitation of friends, and conversation, except religious, worked strangely ill. The prisoners ran away by dozens, preferring the risk of being shot by the guards, to a death served out in inch pieces. Contrary fellows, these convicts! behaving indecently well under the milder regime, following that fanatical report. Absolutely liking to read ; liking their Sabbath-schools and the visits and letters of their friends; not rising in rebellion, as was prophesied, when they saw their warden by the bedside of their sick and dying; but one attempt at escape in all those golden years ; no insurrections ; order and honesty vouched for in the reports as on the increase—practical and convincing proofs these of the determined perversity of the convict mind!

It is refreshing to come to the times when political changes in 1843 raised up new inspectors—"Pharaohs which knew not Joseph," "second Daniels come to judgment," discoursing after this wise : To talk of the power of moral suasion in a community of felons is to talk nonsense. The tiger in his cage may fawn and seem to be subdued, but open his prison door and he is again the tiger of the jungle. To prate about the subduing power of kindness and sympathy is worse than preposterous."

Away went Sunday-school, library, all. The hounds

were to be whipped into submission. The new keepers were men with their eye-teeth cut, and nonsense would not go down with them ; and the convicts, speedily seeing this, settled down into quietness and submission of course ! Such submission as Netherlands yielded Spain, such quietude as that of Italy, such contentment as has anything possessed of a soul not equal parts milk and water under rank injustice (for injustice can be done even a convict), only here it was not virtue, dauntless against tyranny, but evil against evil, devil against devil, and so the conflict lost nobility, and was simply bloody.

Serving out a sentence of fifteen years at that time was one Jim, a fellow who had been captured only after desperate resistance, an excellent specimen of the tiger referred to in the report of 1843 ; an indomitable animal that would not down for flogging, heading every " upstir " and "break out," till the keepers hit on the simple expedient of punishing Jim for every offense committed in his shop. Denial was not listened to ; explanation followed by an increase of punishment. The entrance of several armed keepers grew to be at last $x =$ an unknown quantity of lashes for Jim. Then this tiger bethought himself to do what any other poor hunted creature would, stand at bay. One day he turned on his tormentors, seized a bar of red-hot iron from his forge, dashed in among them, careless of loaded canes and whizzing bullets, knocked down one, half killed another, sent a third scampering for his life, yielded only to overpowering numbers, went to the whipping-post, of course, was tortured till he could bear no more, thrown aside with the threat of another hundred lashes as soon as his back could bear it, and so on in infernal series. Bleeding, fainting, hopeless, God and man seemingly as cold to him as the stones of his cell, the chaplain found him.

Jim's explanation was simple.

"Death from a bullet, I thought, was better than slow torture by the cat. I had done nothing wrong ; I was frantic. I had rather die than live," he whispered faintly.

Meantime the Committee on Punishments were dissatisfied. The reported number of lashes during these three months of terror was enormous, discipline notwithstanding down at the heel and out at elbows, escapes provokingly numerous, and all this bless.d dissatisfaction was light for Jim and others like him. He was allowed an examination, proved innocent, on the whole a decent sort of tiger, as tigers go. In less than a year this desperate ringleader, this incorrigible convict, had the sole charge of making and repairing all the iron bolts used in the Branch Croton Aqueduct, a shop some sixty yards from the prison, and a piece of land allowed him as a garden on the score of merit, and in 1851 he received a pardon, based on the recommendation of the prison authorities.

Damaging a case like that in its tendencies to such reports as that of 1843! in conjunction with others similar, making people ask if, after all, these convicts were not very much as other men are. The officer on night duty, making his rounds, hour after hour, in the grim barred wards, can tell of such sighs and groans, such tears, such restless pacing up and down, as might make you believe there were hearts beating under those striped jackets. One man is beset with fears for his family : "Oh, sir, I have had such a dream about them! For God's sake, try and find out something about them!" —that sounds human ; another is groaning over his guilt ; a third is sure of pardon if his case were but known ; and talking of pardons, one of the merciful ones who remember "the sighing of the prisoner" had once the happiness to carry five pardons to those gloomy walls. Oh! such eyes of entreaty, of hope, of despair, as were turned upon him ! I think it would take us several years of stone everywhere and whitewashed perspective fully to understand their woeful depths.

Among those who flocked about him was an Irishman, a good-natured, broad-shouldered blockhead, who had blundered his way into prison, in spite of the best efforts of his employer, the agent of the Prison Association, and the court itself, to keep him out. He was foremost, his great frame trembling with excitement.

"And is it me pardon that you've brought, your honor?"

"Well, Peter, I'm sorry, but the fact is, the Governor hesitated about granting so many pardons; however, don't be discouraged. Your case is under consideration. You will get it in a month or so."

"Oh! your honor, a month?"

"Well, well, you are sure to get it, you know; it will be sent down."

"But, if your honor had only brought it your own self."

"I know it is hard. I should like to see you out of this myself, and if you would be sensible—I don't know —we might get it in a couple of weeks; but you would be childish over it, I know you would."

"Not I, your honor; don't ye see I'm calm intirely?"

"If I only thought so; I am sorry for you, Peter. Who knows? we might get it sooner—say three or four days; and if you'll be a man about it, I've half a mind to say I'll stay and wait with you till it comes."

"Your honor! your honor! sure I don't know what's come over me, but I can't help misdoubting that ye've got it in your pocket."

"And if I had, now, you wouldn't be childish?"

"Divil a bit, your honor! I'd first say, God bless your honor!—not a word more."

"Well, then, here is your pardon, Peter."

Peter had promised not to be childish, but not a word was said of women, so he fainted, like one, dead away, and there was no small stir to bring him to. This done at last:

"How is this, Peter? I thought you was to be a man."

"I—I—another time, Mr. B.," and he breaks out sobbing.

Lingering doubts still assailed him. He was scarcely yet sure of the blessed news, till he stood on the top of the hill, looking down at the stone walls blinking with their narrow slits of windows, as if they had gone blind, and off at the free river and the purple hills, and all

over these last Freedom was written in such plain hand
that its thought at last found lodgment in his bewil-
dered brain, and thrilled him with an ecstasy ; and,
jumping almost his own height from the ground, and
shouting, " I'm free, Mr. B., I'm free," he started off on
a keen run that never once slackened till he reached the
depot. A vehement, ill-regulated Irishman, but exceed-
ingly humane, and it is comfortable to add that he has
retained to the present day in ᵗhe service and the confidence of his old employers.

· Many such prisoners are tnere ; much foothold is
there for an earnest humanity, not an inch of soil for
the growth of a sentimental interest. The flashy hero-
ine of the sensation story lays aside her velvet dress,
and binds hats and wears hickory like the rest. The
interesting villain walks to dinner with his hands on the
shoulder of some pickpocket or cut-throat. There are
green spots in this stony desert. There is a nursery
where you may see such fair little faces as you kiss
every night in the crib at home ; there are cells gay
with pictures and all manner of rainbow ingenuities,
showing that some of woman's best traits are not yet
crushed out ; yet you have always a sense of an orderly
night-mare strong upon you, and the oppression, and the
instinctive desire to get out, and the growing horror of
but one hour, might and should tell what is the weigh-
ing down of years in that gloomy place.

Now, again, the convicts have their library, the let-
ter-writing, and the visits of their friends, but Sabbath-
schools are discontinued, because convicts are forbidden
to act as teachers, and none others could be obtained.

The reason for such prohibition seems difficult to
comprehend. When the old-fashioned snake-heads did not
work, we tried the T rail, and if Ossa on Pelion of
blankets, and yule fires did not answer with small pox,
we tried fresh air and thin coverings ; but here we have
beings who, following the reversed laws of evil, near the
beast and the savage the higher their degree in
wickedness, and we go on treating them as beasts by
way of making them men. The world bullied and

suspected, and gathered up its skirts as they passed, and so will we, taking them up where society chopped them, at the prison gates. We will never say to ourselves, This is the old system that has worked badly, let us try a new one! What if we could induce this sullen beast to think himself a man, and believe that we believe him so? The Committee of 1839 declared that "convicts were governed, like the rest of mankind, by their mental faculties." Rest of mankind, decent, civilized, virtuous mankind, which binds *you* most effectually—Argus-eyed surveillance or entire confidence? Why, it is Heaven's own magic; it has made giants for the nonce out of moral pigmies, brought great deeds out of small souls. If you are insensible to it, you are behind the convicts, for, on the word of a servant of Christ, so are not they. The teachers selected were necessarily from among the controlling spirits, who influenced their weaker brethren by means of a public opinion, as potent there as inside of prison walls. Not one of these teachers are registered a second time ; not one that did not throw his influence in the scale of good ; not one found, by any breach of trust, forfeiting so rare and sweet a treasure. These be facts, but lest they should be taken, and the causes left, as Utopian (dread word), I will prove them of the same family by Napoleon Buonaparte. That little great man gave most responsible offices to most dangerous men—to keep them quiet. Call him Utopian, not me!

Let us not forget either the serious objection taken on the part of tried and faithful officers, both English and American, to the contract system, a subject, by the the by, to be approached with gingerly caution, for a self-supporting prison economy is the philosopher's stone after which political economists are ever groping. Gradgrind could no further go, this once achieved; it is a thing sacred. What shall be done, then, to the iconoclast, who not only refuses to bow down before the golden image, but even lifts profane hands against it? What can happen, but, entangled in a labyrinth of red tape, to be devoured by a Minotaur of precedent, or to

be cast into a very furnace of indignation ; and yet this
Meloch gorges, the Recording Angel only knows how
many, men, and women's chances for improvement,
hopes of a better life ; forces the less hardened of the
convicts into damaging contact with the oldest ; inter-
feres at every turn with every possible plan for their
bettering ; and yet every true, and pure, and just
sentiment asserts that prisons are sanitary measures,
not speculations ; and if philanthropy is too tame, and
reform too dangerous a name to conjure with, self
interest pleads lest the incendiary's torch should fire
our hearths, the assassin's knife be at our throat ; that
the forty-one thousand and odd arrests that took place
last year in the city of New York alone may not swell
till we are swamped in a second deluge of evil,
smothered with the spreading malaria of sin ; and not
much more worthy than this pitiful economy, of the
magnanimity of a great nation, does it seem to hang
the Damocles sword of our political changes over the
prisoner's scanty feast. If capacity and fitness, not
political creed, are the necessary qualifications of a
prison officer, why should the system that has been
tried and works well be exchanged for at least inex-
perience and its consequent blunders ? "A man who is
cruel," says one, "should enter prison only as a
convict ;" and another, "a man has a right to be common-place in the great desert, but at the head of an
army, or of a gaol to be common-place is an iniquity and
leads to crime," and there is no warrant that the right
man in the right place shall not be exchanged for the
cruel or common-place man. Surely the government has
offices enough within its gift, without the prisoner's
ewe lamb. Surely it behooves that outward Chris-
tianity, and public sentiment that are in reality the
prison-keepers to look well to these things, lest at the
last they should have to offer their Saviour only the
equivocation of Cain : "Am I my brother's keeper ?"

MERCANTILE PRINTING.

WYNKOOP & HALLENBECK,

Book and Job Printers,

NO. 113 FULTON STREET,

NEW YORK.

ALL

KINDS OF PRINTING

EXECUTED AT

SHORT NOTICE,

IN THE

NEATEST STYLE,

AND AT

THE LOWEST CASH PRICES.

POPULAR GOODS

AT

UNION ADAMS',

No. 637 Broadway, N. Y.

——

SHIRTS,   COLLARS,   HOSIERY,

GLOVES, CROQUET STOCKINGS,

CARDIGAN JACKETS,

SCARLET CASHMERE SHIRTS

AND DRAWERS,

ROBES, UMBRELLAS, CANES, SHAWLS,

HOODS, CAPS,

GAITERS, MUFFLERS.

——

DRESS SHIRTS AND COLLARS
MADE TO ORDER.

Late NOVELTIES, from LONDON and PARIS, will be added
to the stock upon the arrival of every steamer.

HUNDERTPFUND & CO.

New York Floral Depot,

No. 947 BROADWAY,

AND

177 FIFTH AVENUE, NEW YORK.

NEW YORK.

BOUQUETS, BASKETS, AND WREATHS FOR WEDDINGS
AND PARTIES MADE OF THE CHOICEST
FLOWERS, AT SHORT NOTICE.

FINE CUT FLOWERS CONSTANTLY ON HAND.

WREATHS AND CROSSES FOR FUNERALS

Made of the choicest White Flowers, at short notice.

IMMORTELLE WREATHS AND CROSSES.

N.B.—Flowers sent to any part of the city or country   Open
from 7 A. M., until 10 P. M.

BOUQUETS from 25 cents to $15.

WOOD BROTHERS,

MANUFACTURERS OF

FINE

PLEASURE CARRIAGES

OF EVERY DESCRIPTION,

No. 596 Broadway, New York.

———◆———

SPECIALITÉ, PARK, AND TOWN CARRIAGES

FOR FAMILY USE.

MERCANTILE
MUTUAL INSURANCE COMPANY,

No. 35 Wall Street, New York.

Assets, January 1, 1866 - - - - $1,366 699

ORGANIZED APRIL, 1844.

The Company has paid to its Customers, up to the present time, Losses amounting to over

EIGHTEEN MILLIONS OF DOLLARS.

For the past nine years the cash dividends paid to Stockholders, made from ONE-THIRD of the net profits, have amounted in the aggregate to

One Hundred and Twenty-one and a Half Per Cent,

Instead of issuing a scrip dividend to dealers, based on the principle that all classes of risks are equally profitable, this Company will hereafter make such cash abatement or discount from the current rates, when premiums are paid, as the general experience of underwriters will warrant, and the net profits remaining at the close of the year will be divided to the Stockholders

This Company continues to make Insurance on Marine and Inland Navigation and Transportation Risks, on the most favorable terms, including Risks on Merchandise of all kinds, Hulls and Freight.

Policies issued making loss payable in Gold or Currency, at the OFFICE in NEW YO..K, or in Sterling, at the OFFICE of RATHBONE BROTHERS & Co., in LIVERPOOL.

TRUSTEES.

LIFE INSURANCE.

THE

Manhattan Life Insurance Company.

Office 156 and 158 Broadway, New York.

Cash Capital and accumulation over $2,250,000; deposited with the Comptroller of the State, for the security of all Policy Holders, $100,000.

Policies issued on the most favorable terms. Prospectus of the Company, with every information, can be gratuitously obtained at the office of the Company, or at the Agencies.

C. Y. WEMPLE,
Secretary.

HENRY STOKES,
President.

ABRAM DUBOIS, M.D., at the office daily, from 2 to 4 o'clock, P.M.

Annuities granted, payable in all the principal cities of the United States and Canada, and in London, Paris, and Amsterdam.

DIRECTORS:

Henry Van Schaick,	Henry Stokes,	Edmund Coffin,
A. C. Kingsland,	Eleazer Parmly,	James C. Baldwin,
Philip Reynolds,	Henry A. Kerr,	Daniel Burtnett,
John T. Terry,	Edwin J. Brown,	John S. Harris,
Wm. K. Strong,	Jas. M. Benedict,	Edward Schell,
Jas. Van Norden,	James Stokes,	Denton Pearsall,
Edward Haight,	Jas. M. LeLean,	E. W. Blatchford,
Wm. J. Valentine,	Leonard M. Thorne,	Robert S. Bussing,
Samuel C. Reed,	D. Henry Haight,	Alwyn A. Alvord,
C. Y. Wimple,	John D. Russ,	James E. Yeatman,
Albert Clark,	Lewis B. Loder,	Henry Simons,
John S. Williams,	John W. Hunter,	John Anderson.

BRADY'S

National Photographic Gallery,

No. 785 BROADWAY, N. Y.

(Cor. Tenth st., opposite Grace Church.)

———•◆•———

Mr. BRADY begs to announce that his Gallery is replete with an almost complete collection of every prominent person and every celebrated scene and incident connected with the late war, forming, in fact, a pictorial history of the troublous scenes through which the Nation has just passed, especially interesting to the student and the patriot.

———

Mr. BRADY has devoted special attention to pictures upon

PORCELAIN,

and has succeeded, after much labor and expense, in producing specimens unrivaled in their finish, and superior to the most perfect water-color portraits.

The Imperial Photographs, by Mr. BRADY, still retain the excellence so long accorded to them, whether finished in India Ink or Water Color.

———————

THE OIL PAINTINGS

emanating from Mr. BRADY's Gallery, receive the same degree of attention as heretofore; and the copying of old portraits, paintings. &c., is made a special branch of business.

THE ANNUAL REPORT OF THE DIRECTORS

OF

The Ninth National Bank

TO THE STOCKHOLDERS.

———◆•◆———

NEW YORK, January 9, 1866.

The election was held this day, and the Directors were unanimously re-elected for the ensuing year. For this renewed and flattering expression of confidence on the part of the Stockholders, the Directors return their thanks.

During the fiscal year we have paid two Dividends of FIVE per cent. each, and the government taxes.

And now exhibit an actual SURPLUS, over and above all losses expenses, and dividends, of NINETEEN per cent. on the CAPITAL STOCK.

From the earnings of the last six months we have applied $50,000, that is, Five per cent. on the Capital Stock, to the extinguishment of the premium account; and although the Stockholders do not get this Five per cent. in a dividend, yet it is represented in the United States Stocks held by the Bank.

During the past year your Bank became a member of the New York Clearing House Association, by a unanimous vote of that body.

We are able to report that your Bank has well fulfilled its patriotic mission, of aiding the placing of the Government Loans. The amount of subscriptions to the Seven-Thirties was Forty-three Million Two Hundred and Sixty-two Thousand Three Hundred Dollars ($43,262,300), this being the largest subscription taken by any one bank. To appreciate this result, we would remark that, had nineteen other banks taken each the same amount, the whole loan would have been taken by the twenty.

This gives us opportunity to say that, having served our beloved country in its hour of peril, we desire now to turn all our efforts to the securing in all legitimate and honorable ways the increase of our business with the community; to that end we invite the cordial co-operation of each Stockholder.

Our organization is now so well perfected as to give us all much satisfaction, and the relief from so much government business gives our officers time to attend to individual dealers.

We receive the deposits of the business community, and we hold ourselves in readiness to DISCOUNT GOOD BUSINESS PAPER, payable at short dates. Such paper, being based on the sale of commodities, is, in our opinion, the safest business a bank can do. We continue to buy and sell Government Stocks.

JOSEPH U. ORVIS, President.
JOHN T. HILL, Cashier.

C. O. STEVENS & CO.,

Jewellers and Silversmiths,

No. 38 East Fourteenth street,

UNION SQUARE, NEW YORK.

A CHOICE SELECTION OF

FRENCH CLOCKS, BRONZES,

AND

PORCELAIN GOODS.

BARGAINS

IN

CHINA, GLASS, &C.

---

100 SETS FINE AMERICAN RICH CUT AND ENGRAVED GLASS, 12 GOBLETS, 12 CHAMPAGNES, 12 WINES, 12 HOCKS, 2 DECANTERS, 12 FINGER BOWLS WITH "INITIALS" TO ORDER, $60 per set.

100 GOLD BAND FRENCH CHINA TEA SETS, 44 PIECES, $16 per set.

100 FANCY FRENCH CHINA TEA SETS, 44 PIECES, $20 to $25 per set.

50 DECORATED DINNER SETS, ON EXTRA QUALITY FINE PARISIAN GRANITE, 189 PIECES, $125 per set.

100 WHITE FINE PARISIAN GRANITE DINNER SETS, 138 PIECES, $35 per set.

200 DOZEN WHITE FRENCH CHINA DESSERT PLATES, $2 per dozen.

100 WHITE FRENCH CHINA DINNER SETS, SECOND SELECTION, 141 PIECES $36 per set.

CHANDELIERS, SILVER PLATED WARE, &c., AT MODERATE PRICES.

Persons furnishing either for city or country use will do well to examine these goods.

E. V. HAUGHWOUT & CO.,

Nos. 488, 490, and 492 Broadway.

CORNER OF BROOME STREET.

EDWARD McGILL,

GENTLEMEN'S

HATTER & OUTFITTER,

643 BROADWAY,

Corner Bleecker Street.   **NEW YORK.**

———•••———

DEALERS IN

LADIES' AND GENTLEMEN'S FINE FURS

BOYS' HATS, UMBRELLAS, CANES, &c.

WELLS & BONTECOU,

(Old Firm—Baker, Wells & Co.),

LUMBER DEALERS,

WHOLESALE AND RETAIL.

ESTABLISHED 1839.

YARDS—On West Street, between Houston and King, and Houston and Clarkson Streets, and Nos. 572 and 574 Washington Street.

STEAM MILL,

WASHINGTON STREET, Corner of CLARKSON.

Yard Office, No. 344 West Street,

Down-Town Office, 47 South Street.

The particular attention of SHIPPERS and COUNTRY DEALERS is respectfully invited to our large first-class and well-assorted STOCK OF LUMBER, including SCANTLING, SHINGLES, YELLOW-PINE FLOORING, STEP PLANK, &c., &c.

A REMEDY FOR CHOLERA.

DETROIT, MICH., Dec. 13, 1865.

BROTHER—In view of the approach of the cholera season I send you for the O. F. a receipt for cholera syrup, which I have used as a family medicine, for all diseases of the bowels, for over twenty years, and in past cholera seasons, with good effect:

> 2 oz. Tincture of Myrrh,
>
> "   Capsicum,
>
> " Essence of Peppermint,
>
> ½ "   " Cinnamon,
>
> 1 gill best Brandy.

In an attack of the cholera I should give from a tablespoon to half a wine-glass in half a teacup of hot water. Soak the feet in hot water with some Cayenne pepper in it, and apply a mustard plaster to the stomach ; or what is better (if it can be obtained), steeped smart-weed put on the stomach as hot as it can be borne.

The dose can be repeated in from half an hour to an hour, according to the nature of the attack. It warms and invigorates the whole system, and in eight cases out of ten, if taken in time, no further medical attendance will be required.

Though I would not advise a perfect reliance on this prescription, yet I would use it in the absence of a physician, as a means of checking and giving relief, and if not needed when he comes, so much the better. Taken in doses of from one to three teaspoonfuls in half a cupful of hot water (and repeated according to circumstances), it is a sovereign remedy for all diseases of the bowels, and no family testing it will ever be without it.

Fraternally, yours,

J O. MELICK.

www.ingramcontent.com/pod-product-compliance
Lightning Source LLC
Chambersburg PA
CBHW031439270326
41930CB00007B/779

*9 7 8 3 7 4 4 6 9 2 0 5 2 *